Get Fit Through Power Walking!

"Power walk your way to better health with Becky Youman's great tips!" – Dr. Carey Windler, president of the Texas Orthopedic Association, and Sports Medicine physician for the University of Texas Athletic Department

D1206436

About the Author

Becky Youman is a published author, certified Personal Trainer and an avid walker. In addition, she is also a certified yoga instructor. She combines a wealth of knowledge on walking, fitness and nutrition with the proven ability to write in a way that her readers understand and appreciate. Her other books include *Mountain Biking Central Texas*; now in its fifth edition, *Chile Guide*; and *Ecuador & Galapagos Guide.* She can be found power walking, training, and teaching yoga in Lampasas, Texas when not trekking around Latin America.

Get Fit Through Power Walking!

Becky Youman

Cold Spring Press

Cold Spring Press

P.O. Box 284, Cold Spring Harbor, NY 11724
E-mail: Jopenroad@aol.com

Copyright©2003 by Becky Youman
All Rights Reserved

ISBN 1-892975-89-0
Library of Congress Control Number: 2003104438

Acknowledgements

I'd like to acknowledge and thank Dr. Carey Windler for his input with this book. My husband, Bryan Estep, deserves kudos and thanks for his careful reading and editing of the manuscript. Jonathan Stein, my publisher, gets a big *gracias* as well. Lastly, I applaud the Raisin for walking with me every single step along the way.

Disclaimer

The author and publisher have made every effort to ensure the accuracy of information contained in this book, but can accept no liability for any loss, injury or inconvenience sustained by anybody as a result of information or advice contained here. Readers are responsible for having any exercise program approved by their physician before beginning.

Table of Contents

Sidebars, Charts & Logs

1. Introduction

Imagine if someone came to you with a product that would help you lose weight, reduce your risk of disease, decrease your stress levels and improve your mental clarity. Sounds pretty good, doesn't it? Now imagine if this great product were available for the low price of a pair of walking shoes. Sounding even better, right? Well, that's what's being offered here.

Walking truly is a wonder product. It's an inexpensive, easy to master, portable, and fun way to incorporate movement into your daily life. A regular walking program can reduce your risk of heart disease, high blood pressure, diabetes and certain types of cancer. It can also help you reach or maintain a healthy weight, increase your strength, and reduce tension.

This book will show you how to **get fit through power walking** by creating the program that's right for you. Whether you're new to fitness activities, a runner whose joints can no longer take pounding the pavement, or even somebody who already walks on a regular basis, you will benefit from the time-tested information presented here. Although most of us have known how to walk since we were about a year old, walking for fitness, also known as power walking, is another matter. I'll guide you through the specific techniques needed to walk fast enough to reap health benefits. You'll also learn about preventing injuries; walking safety; and the advantages of cross training. I even include a chapter on issues relevant to women walkers.

Many of you may be thinking about walking as a tool for reaching your healthy weight. It's important to understand that your eating habits play a key role in walking for weight-loss. I'll guide you through a walker's nutrition plan as well as offer tips for incorporating this plan into your daily meals.

Walking really can change your life. With the programs and structure provided, all you have to do is put one foot in front of the other. Let's get started today!

2. Why Walk?

Why Walk?

People in this country don't move much anymore. Inactivity has become programmed into our lives. We spend most of our day in the car and at the office. When we get home, remote controls, riding lawn mowers and other modern conveniences ensure that we exert as little energy as possible. We have become scarily sedentary.

This situation has prompted the Center for Disease Control to call physical inactivity a "serious, nationwide problem." There is a huge cost associated with the unnecessary illnesses and premature deaths that are caused by our country's sluggishness. A Boston hospital estimated the figure at 24 billion dollars. Imagine the many positive ways our country could use that 24 billion dollars if people became more active.

You can't take responsibility for the entire country, but by using this book and starting a walking plan, you are taking responsibility for yourself. Congratulations. Power walking will bring improvements to many areas of your life. The benefits of making a commitment to becoming moderately active on a regular basis are so numerous it's almost hard to believe.

Reduced Risk of Disease

Walking can reduce the risk of many life-threatening diseases. Recent studies have shown that moderate intensity walking can:

- Reduce the risk of heart disease by 30-40%
- Reduce the risk of developing diabetes by 50%
- Reduce the risk of some kinds of cancer (colon, prostate, breast)
- Reduce the risk of developing high blood pressure
- Reduce the risk of stroke
- Reduce the risk of developing osteoporosis

Improved Physical Health

While reduced risk of disease motivates some people, others are more interested in the improvements that walking can make to their physical health. Again, the benefits of power walking are many:

- Builds bone density
- Develops strong muscles and joints
- Reduces stiffness in joints
- Reduces LDL (bad) cholesterol levels
- Raises HDL (good) cholesterol levels
- Helps condition lungs
- Improves circulation

Weight Control

One of the side effects of our country's inactivity is that we have become increasingly overweight. A Center for Disease Control survey shows that 61% of Americans are either overweight (10% above normal body weight) or obese (20% above normal body weight.) In addition to all the benefits listed above, walking can help you attain and maintain your optimal weight.

I'll cover Walking for Weight Loss more in a later chapter, but the most important thing to understand is that walking helps you control your weight in a number of ways:

- Burns calories
- Preserves and builds lean muscle mass
- Helps with appetite control

Improved Well-Being

The benefits of walking extend beyond physical improvements. A regular walking program can also affect your general well-being. Power walking increases the flow of blood and oxygen to the brain, as well as stimulates the release of certain beneficial hormones. This can have many positive effects. Some of these include:

- Increased energy levels
- Better sleep
- Reduced feelings of anxiety or depression
- Increased alertness
- Stress release

Because You Like It

It's all well and good to list the reasons that walking is good for you. In fact, you probably already knew quite a few of them. Those reasons might get you started on a walking program, but you won't stay with it unless you like it.

Make this commitment to yourself – "I will stick with my walking program for three months." After three months you will have started to incorporate walking into your daily life. You'll become "addicted" to the energy boost and equanimity that walking provides. In fact, over time you'll start to feel poorly if you don't walk or get some other form of exercise.

At that point, you'll be walking because you want to. You'll count on it to help you burn off steam when you're feeling stressed, energize you when you're dragging, give you thinking time when you need to contemplate an issue in your life, or provide you a place to go off into your own little world when you need some space. You won't be walking because somebody told you that you should, you'll be walking because you like it.

3. Get Started

Shoes

One of the great things about walking is that it takes so little equipment. All you really need is a good pair of walking shoes. These shoes are important however. Don't scrimp on them. It's worth the $50 for a decent walking-specific pair. Proper fitting walking shoes will help you walk faster, avoid injury and be much more comfortable.

Walking Shoe Design

Walking-specific shoes are designed to help propel you forward while causing minimum impact to your body. A good walking shoe will be flexible in the front part of the shoe so that your foot can bend at the ball as you rock forward. It will also have a low (no more than one inch high), rounded heel. This will provide cushioning while still allowing for a good heel strike. This design leads to an easy heel-to-toe motion during your stride. A good pair of walking shoes will also be lightweight and made from materials that breathe.

There are categories of shoes for categories of feet. That means that certain walking shoes are designed for specific users or to correct specific foot problems. For example, heavy walkers, walkers with flat feet, or people who over-pronate (ankles roll exaggeratedly in when they walk due to collapsed arches) can often benefit from shoes

> ### RUN AWAY FROM RUNNING SHOES
> People are often tempted to use that old pair of running shoes they have in the closet rather than invest in a new pair of walking shoes. Don't do it! Most running shoes, thick at the heel and stiff at the toe-box, have a much higher platform than walking shoes. They won't evenly support your stride and will invariably lead to shin splints. They will kill your walking program before it really gets a chance to begin.

designed for motion control with a firm heel counter. People with high arches should look for a more cushioned shoe. Mid-weight walkers with no specific foot problems can use a general walking shoe designed with good stability yet flexibility at the ball. With all the variety available, you can see that it's important to buy the shoe that's been designed for walkers with feet like yours.

Proper Fit

The best way to find a shoe that's right for your foot is to seek out a professional. If you're lucky enough to live in a town with a walking specialty store, you can do that easily. The staff will be well versed on the benefits of each brand and model of shoe. By taking into account your stride, weight, foot position and usage, they can help you target the perfect pair for your needs.

Realistically, I know that some of you don't have access to a specialty store. Don't let that be an excuse to delay your walking program. Most general sporting goods stores display their shoes by intended sex and specific sport. Find the men's or women's walking shoe section and start trying them on. You can find a very good walking shoe in the $50-$80 range. It's been my experience that the marginal benefit of the super-expensive pair of shoes does not outweigh the additional cost. The best values are those in the $50-$80 range.

There are some easy strategies, passed to me by the experts at WalkTex in Austin, which you can follow to help ensure your shoes will fit properly after you carry them out of the store.

- **Try on a number of pairs**. Even a well-designed shoe might not be comfortable on your feet. It's important to try on a number of pairs to find the one that feels good to you. Always try the shoes on both feet. Many people have one foot that is a bit larger than the other, so trying on both shoes can make a difference. Also, no matter how pressed you are for time, be sure to lace both shoes up completely. You'd be amazed how much more you can tell about a shoe's comfort when it is fully laced. If any part of the shoe rubs your foot, opt for another pair. Don't think that you will "break a shoe in." The single most important thing about any walking shoe is that it be comfortable from the get go.

- **Bring your athletic socks**. Dress socks or hose are much thinner than athletic socks. Make sure you try your shoes on with the socks that you'll be wearing when you walk.

THE WALKING SHOE WORK-OVER
Before you even try on a pair of shoes you want to make sure it can pass the Walking Shoe Work-Over.

- **Press** – Place the shoe on the ground and press your finger into the toe of the shoe. The heel should come off the ground.

- **Bend** – Bend the toe of the shoe up towards the heel. Make sure the shoe bends at the ball of the foot, not at the arch.

- **Wring** – Grab the shoe with one hand at the ball and the other at the heel and twist your hands as if you were wringing out a wet towel. The shoe should twist slightly.

- **Shop in the evening**. Exercise tends to cause your feet to swell. If you shop for shoes in the morning, your feet will be at their smallest. The shoes that feel great in the store might feel tight and pinched after a walk. If you shop for shoes in the afternoon, when you've spent more time on your feet, you'll get a better idea of what the shoes will really feel like during your walk.

- **Let fit, not size, be your guide**. Many people wear walking shoes that are a larger size than their dress shoes. You need to make sure that you have a thumb's width of room between your longest toe and the end of the shoe. Because you're wearing athletic socks and your feet are swollen, your feet are going to take up more space than they usually do. Don't be vain about your shoe size — you'll really suffer if you are.

- **Try on a number of brands**. Don't let advertising lead to you one brand over another. Test a number of brands and decide for yourself which ones are the most comfortable on your feet. Again, your comfort is paramount.

AVOIDING BLISTERS

Nothing can stop your walking program faster than a huge eruption on your heel. For those of you with tender feet, avoiding blisters will be a top priority. Staying away from cotton socks or wearing a silk sock liner should be your first line of defense. If you're still feeling friction, you can lube up your feet with petroleum jelly. (It sounds hot and squishy, but it's not.)

If you start to feel a "hot spot," a point of friction, you'll want to treat it immediately before it becomes a full-fledged blister. Cover the spot with a Band-Aid, moleskin, or Compeed (available at drugstores) until it is no longer tender.

• **Take a test ride**. Once you've found a pair that feels good to you, take a brisk walk around the store. It's important that the shoe is tested under the conditions in which it will be used. Make sure that the heel doesn't slip and that your foot doesn't rub anywhere.

Timely Replacement

Over time your shoes will compress and compact, meaning they will no longer offer you the support you need. This can lead to injury. The experts at WalkTex suggest that you replace your walking shoes every six months or 400 miles, whichever comes first.

Don't assume that you can just look at your shoe and tell whether or not it needs replacing. The midsoles at the points of impact can breakdown and lose their cushioning and you won't even see it. This can lead to painful shinsplints. It's much better for your feet for you to buy a $50 pair of shoes and replace them every six months than it is to buy a $100 pair and wait a year to replace them.

CIAO TO CHAFFING

There's not much worse than chaffed skin while you're walking. Chaffing, caused by clothing or skin rubbing against other skin, is a common problem and easily avoidable. Look for clothes with flat seams that are less likely to rub and irritate your skin. If your thighs are rubbing together, you might want to invest in a pair of long Lycra shorts.

If you still find that you're chaffing, use a lubricant to help dissipate friction. Petroleum jelly is a cheap, easy to find option. If you find it too greasy, there are lighter exercise-specific lubricants available like Body Glide and Chafe-Eez that can be found in running stores. These same lubricants can be used on your feet to help avoid blisters.

Socks

Many people do just fine with cotton-blend athletic socks, as long as they fit well and don't bunch up in their shoes. If you find that you're getting blisters, however, you'll want to "up-grade" your socks. Synthetic materials such as CoolMax and Dri-Fit wick moisture away from your feet, helping prevent the softening of the skin that is the first step in blister formation. Wool does the job as well. Thorlo and SmartWool both make excellent, albeit expensive socks. If you're getting blisters through, believe me, it's worth it.

Another option is to wear a silk sock liner underneath your regular socks. That way the friction rubs between the two pairs of socks rather than between the cotton-blend sock and your skin. You can find both walking socks and sock liners at general athletic stores.

Clothing

The beauty of walking is that all you really need is a good pair of shoes and socks that don't give you blisters. You can basically wear anything you find comfortable and non-constricting.

If you're on a tight budget, spend the money on shoes and walk in clothes that are already in your closet. Many people are fine with t-shirts and shorts in warm weather and a sweatsuit when it gets cooler. Don't let a lack of high-tech clothing be an excuse for not starting your walking program.

Some of you, however, may want to expand your walking wardrobe. Specialized synthetic textiles, materials that breathe, and quick drying fabrics can increase your comfort level as you battle the elements. There's no need to go out and buy everything at once. You can pick up an article of clothing every couple of months and end up with a walking wardrobe that's right for you. That windbreaker you buy to reward yourself for sticking to your walking program for eight weeks will end up being meaningful as well as useful.

Layering

Your clothing will vary greatly depending on the climate and time of year. One of the keys to comfort is proper layering. Depending on the weather conditions, you may wear one, two, three, or even four layers of clothing. The more extreme the temperatures, the more specialized your apparel should be.

Warm Weather Clothing

You'll generally only need one layer of clothing in warm weather conditions. A comfortable, light-colored, t-shirt and pair of shorts will do just fine. If it is especially warm or humid, you might want to invest in clothing with fabrics, like CoolMax and Dri-Fit, that wick sweat away from the skin. It won't make you walk faster, but it will make you more comfortable and help prevent chafing.

A good hat is a must in hot weather. Make sure the bill is large enough to shade your face from direct sunlight. Light colors are good here too.

Cold Weather Clothing

Layering and clothing materials become more important as the weather gets cooler. When it's cool outside, wicking fabrics as your *base layer* really do make a difference. I'm especially prone to becoming chilled once my clothes get wet. As a result, I make sure that the layer of clothing against my body is made of some type of synthetic fabric, like polypropylene, that pulls sweat away from my skin. Cotton material is a no-no as a base layer in cooler weather.

Your second layer in cool weather is known as the *insulating layer*. It helps keep you warm. Depending on the conditions, this layer could be a long-sleeve t-shirt, a fleece, a pair of sweat pants, or some running tights. It's up to you to avoid overheating by removing this layer before you start to sweat too much. If you get cool, simply put this layer back on.

The *outer layer* is designed to protect you against the climate conditions, be it wind, rain, snow or sleet. In cooler weather, a light windbreaker will usually be sufficient. If it's raining, an outer layer that keeps water out but lets perspiration pass through can make a huge difference in your comfort level. Materials like Gortex are expensive, but they are worth it if you live in a rainy area. You can usually find some great deals on clothes made from Gortex and other similar materials at sierratradingpost.com.

Putting on a hat and gloves in cooler weather will allow you to wear less clothing on your body. It's also easier to stick a pair of gloves in your pocket than to tie a sweatshirt around your waist when you start to warm up.

Windy, Wet, or Very Cold Weather Clothing

When the weather starts to get more extreme your clothing can make a huge difference. A non-cotton, wicking base layer is tremendously important in very cold weather. Your insulating layer may need to be thicker in cold weather, or you might even want two insulating layers, such a fleece vest and a long-sleeved fleece. A high-quality outer layer that stops both wind and rain from penetrating to your insulating layer will make you a happy walker.

You can lose up to 30% of your body heat through the surface area of your head. With that in mind, a wool or synthetic cap is paramount in extremely cold weather. Wearing dark colors that absorb sunlight is also helpful, as long as you're not walking at dusk.

Safety Clothing

If you are going to be walking at dusk or dark, it's important that you do everything possible to be seen by passing motorists. Many shoes and jackets now come with reflective materials. If you're walking on the streets early, before the sun comes up, or after dark, it's really worth investing $10-$15 in a reflective safety vest to give yourself the best chance of being seen.

Another option is a flashing red light. Found in sporting goods stores, often in the bike section, these lights can be attached to your clothes or worn on a band around your arm to make yourself even more visible.

Walking Accessories, Gadgets and Gizmos

Some of the items sold as walking accessories are absolutely superfluous, but others can come in quite handy. Remember, not one of these items is necessary to begin a walking program. They do make good rewards though. Think of using them to motivate yourself to stick to your plan.

Pedometers

If I were to recommend just one accessory, it would be a pedometer. They are an inexpensive ($20-$50) and invaluable tool in tracking how much movement you get over the course of a day. I'll cover their use in the Walking for Weight Loss Plan, but outline the important variables to look for when buying a pedometer here.

A pedometer, worn at the waist, has an internal mechanism that registers every time your hip moves in the walking motion. It basically counts the number of steps you take while wearing the device. The most basic models simply count steps. Fancier models will also calculate miles walked (based on a stride length that you enter), as well as calories burned. As far as counting steps go, pedometers are very accurate. When it gets to miles and calories burned there are still many improvements to be made. I recommend sticking with the most basic models because step counting is really what you should focus on.

When buying a pedometer, there are a few features that are very important. Make sure that you can read the pedometer without unclipping it from your belt or pants. You also want to check that it has a strap to attach the pedometer to your belt loop so that it doesn't end up flipping into the toilet when you go to the bathroom. My favorite brand is the Accusplit Eagle series (www.accusplit.com). The New Lifestyles Digiwalker SW series is also excellent (www.digiwalker.com).

Fanny Packs

Some people don't like to have anything in their hands or pockets when they walk, but they like to bring along some water or food or have a place to stash keys and a windbreaker. This is where a walking-specific fanny pack can come in handy. Look for a pack that sits firmly on your hips and doesn't bounce around when you walk. You also want to make sure that your hands and arms don't hit the pack during your walking stride.

Hydration Packs

Another option for carrying your water and gear is a hydration pack. Built like small backpacks, they have removable interior bladders that you can fill with water or whatever drink you prefer. An over-the-shoulder straw system allows you to drink without breaking your stride. Many of the packs also have extra pockets for stashing your additional gear. Examples of popular brands include Camelbak, Kelty, and Platypus.

Walking Poles

Walking poles, commonly used in Europe, are starting to catch on in the U.S. as well. There are a number of benefits to walking with poles. They absorb some of the shock of your steps and distribute your weight more evenly, which is good for your knees and back. They are especially nice for overweight people who might suffer from joint pain walking without sticks. Studies show that you burn about 20% more calories when you walk with poles because you are getting your upper body involved as well as your legs.

I don't use poles when I walk in town, but consider them essential for hiking. They tremendously help take strain off my knees when going both up and downhill. I also get a great upper body and ab workout when I use them to hike up steep hills.

There are a variety of poles available. They range from simple models to ultra-light titanium with shock absorbers. You'll want to make sure that the grip is comfortable in your hands. I suggest buying ones that can be adjusted to different heights so that you can make concessions to going up and down hill. The website www.sierratradingpost.com usually carries some very high quality poles at discounted prices. You can also buy them at outdoor and sporting goods stores.

Heart Rate Monitors

Heart rate monitors are a great tool for people looking to make real gains in their cardiorespiratory fitness. They can be expensive however, so I don't recommend them for beginner walkers unless your doctor has advised you to keep your heart rate below a certain level. I cover their use in the Walking for Fitness Plan, but will go over some of their features here.

The most accurate heart rate monitors come in two parts. The first part is a strap that goes around your chest. Your heart rate is detected by mechanisms on the strap that transmit the information via an electric signal to a watch on your wrist.

Heart rate monitor models range from the simple (about $50) to the ultra complex (upwards of $400.) The simple models basically show only your current heart rate on the watch display. Midrange models will not only show your heart rate, but will also beep at you if your rate falls out of the desired range you have entered for that particular workout. They might also display an average heart rate at the end of your workout. The wrist monitor will usually include a watch and timer on the mid-range models. The high-end models, unnecessary for most walkers, are like personal trainers. They download data to your computer, track nutrition, and store a wide range of information about your workouts.

I recommend a midrange model. My favorite manufacturer of heart rate monitors is Polar (www.polarusa.com), and my recommended model for walkers is the A5. Cardiosport (www.cardiosport.com) also makes a high quality range of products. You can buy heart rate monitors in almost any sporting goods store.

4. Choose Your Plan & Stick With It!

Now that you've got your shoes and any other equipment you might want, it's time to develop a walking program that's right for you. Each person who uses this book will start at a different fitness level and have unique goals. The aim of this chapter is to help you determine your starting point so that you can choose the proper plan for your specific objectives.

Precautions

It's easy to get excited about starting your walking program and accidentally push yourself too hard at the beginning. As difficult as it may be to contain yourself, please start slowly so you don't get burned out, overly sore, or even injured. You've got to give your body time to adjust to the new demands that you are placing on it.

Of course anybody with health problems, including but not limited to heart disease, high cholesterol, high blood pressure, diabetes, or obesity, should consult a physician before beginning an exercise program. Smokers, people with a family history of disease, and those with a sedentary lifestyle are advised to consult a doctor as well. Even healthy men and women who want to begin a vigorous program would be wise to consult a physician first.

The Program for You

It's important to know your intent before you begin your program. In fact, you have to know the desired outcome of your walking plan before you can choose the proper one for your goals. I have outlined four general plans in this book. Each plan demands a different level of intensity. It's important to start with the appropriate plan for your fitness level. Nothing will burn you out or get you injured faster than trying to take on more than you can handle.

Plan One: Getting Started

If you have not been exercising previously, you'll want to begin with the **Starter Plan**. Once you have completed this plan you can move on to the Improved Health Plan.

Plan Two: Improved Health

Studies have shown that as little as 30-minutes a day of physical activity can lead to huge improvements in health. As outlined in Chapter Two, walking can reduce the risk of heart disease, of developing diabetes, of certain types of cancer, of developing high blood pressure, of stroke, and of high cholesterol. It can also improve your mental health by reducing stress and increasing energy levels. If you already engage in some activity and your goal is simply to improve your health, you should begin with the **Improved Health Plan**.

Plan Three: Improved Fitness

While health improvements can be achieved with as little as 30-minutes a day of moderate activity, fitness gains require more than that. Better cardio-vascular fitness requires increasing both the intensity level and duration of your workout – power walking. It's important that you be able to easily complete the last week of the Improved Health Plan before moving on the **Improved Fitness Plan**.

Plan Four: Weight Loss

Walking for weight loss requires the commitment of daily exercise combined with a healthy eating plan. Long-term dietary modifications and an active lifestyle will help you achieve your healthy weight. See the **Weight Loss Plan** for more details.

Goals

While each of these plans describes a general intent, it's important to have both short and long-term goals that are achievable and measurable. It's through reaching these goals that you will feel the sense of accomplishment that will keep you on your plan. Goals will vary widely from person to person. Some possible goals include:

• Getting in good enough shape to walk a 10k
• Completing at least 85% of your scheduled workouts per week
• Walking a certain number of miles or minutes a month
• Dropping down to a smaller clothing size
• Decreasing your body fat percentage
• Walking a marathon (hey, you never know!)
• Decreasing your one-mile walk time by a minute

THE TEN-MINUTE PLEDGE

There are occasional days when the last thing in the world I want to do is go for a walk. I make the commitment to myself to walk for at least ten minutes on those days. By telling myself that I can quit walking after ten minutes if I want to, I know I have an out. I'm amazed at how often, after getting myself out the door and warmed up, I want to continue walking. If I don't want to keep walking after ten minutes, I quit because I know it's what my body is telling me to do.

Motivating Yourself

Regardless of your motivation level when starting out the program, there will be days when you don't want to continue. You might be discouraged because you feel like you're not making progress towards your goals, you might feel overwhelmed with other commitments, or you might just feel lazy. All of those feelings are natural and valid, but you can't let them derail you.

The sad fact is that 50% of people who start an exercise program quit within six months. There are lots of things you can do to make sure you're not in that "drop out" group. Here are some of the ones that I've found helpful.

Walk with a Friend. While you might not feel bad bagging out on yourself, leaving your friend high and dry is another matter all together. You'll be much less likely to hit that snooze button if you know that somebody is waiting and depending on you. Studies have shown that people who have a friend or family member included in their commitment to exercise generally stick with their walking programs better than people who don't.

Walk in the Morning. Getting up an hour earlier than you are accustomed might seem like a form of torture, but it's one way to make sure that lagging motivation and tempting alternatives don't sabotage your walking plan. In the morning the only other option you're tempted by is sleep. If you wait to walk until evening, there are all sorts of activities that can lure you away from your plan...dinner dates, movies, parties, errand running, or even working late might seem more important than hitting the street.

That doesn't mean that people who walk in the evening are doomed to failure, but there are many more potential roadblocks. If you're a morning walker it's a good idea to lay out your clothes the previous evening. Your clothes will serve as a reminder of your morning plans before you go to sleep and you won't have to think when you roll out of bed the next day.

SAMPLE CONTRACT

I, Wendy Walker, being of sound mind and body that gets sounder by the day, pledge to adhere to the following walking workout plan for the next four weeks.

My Commitment: I will walk for the following amount of time each day at 6:30am:

	M	T	W	Th	F	S	Su
Week 1	30 min.	30 m	30 m	30 m	30 m	off	30 m
Week 2	30 m	30 m	30 m	30 m	30 m	30 m	off
Week 3	40 m	40 m	40 m	40 m	40 m	off	40 m
Week 4	40 m	40 m	40 m	40 m	40 m	40 m	off

Partner's Commitment: Hugh Helper, my early-rising husband, will assist me by getting up and turning on the bedroom lights when the alarm goes off.

My Reward: Hugh will buy me that cool pedometer I've been wanting if I successfully complete at least 21 of my 24 workouts.

Paying the Consequences: If I don't complete at least 21 of my walking workouts I will do the dishes by myself every night for two weeks.

Date: _____
Review Date: _____
My Signature: _____
Partner's Signature: _____

Walk at Lunch. If you can't stand the idea of getting up early, walking during your lunch hour is another good option. Turning people down when they ask you if you want to join them for lunch will feel awkward at first, but soon it will be considered a given at the office that you're a lunch walker. In fact, once you establish the fact that you're using your lunch hour for exercise, a funny thing will happen: your workmates will expect you to walk. That little bit of peer pressure may do just the trick on those days that your motivation levels are low. You might also find that others will join you.

When I worked in an office, I bought an extra pair of walking shoes and keep them, along with a few pairs of socks, some t-shirts, and a windbreaker, in a duffle bag under my desk. That way I didn't have to worry about forgetting my shoes or not having the proper gear.

Write a Contract. One thing you can do to keep yourself accountable is to create a contract with a friend or relative concerning your walking plan. In this contract you will state your commitment very specifically. The other person, your partner for the contract, will also have specific commitments. You will establish a time period for the contract as well as specific rewards and consequences. At the end of the time period you will evaluate how you did. If you reached your contract goal, you will reward yourself. If not, you'll have to pay the consequences.

Sign up for an Event. Signing up to walk a 5k or 10k can be a great motivator. You might have a goal simply to finish, or you may determine a specific time goal for the event.

Vary Your Walking Route. I used to walk at lunch on a beautiful beach in California, but even that sight got old after doing the same thing day after day. Every once in a while I would cruise through the neighborhood around my office instead of going to the beach simply to enjoy a change of scenery. You can also walk your regular route in the opposite direction to shake things up a little. It's amazing how many new things you'll notice when you're walking on the other side of the street.

Subscribe to Fitness Magazines. Magazines like Health, Fitness, and Shape (for women) and Men's Health and Men's Journal are great monthly motivators. Although not focused exclusively on walking, they often cover walking as well as offer other fitness and nutrition tips. The more you can educate yourself on physical fitness and how your body works, the greater chance you have of sticking to your plan.

Schedule Your Workouts like Appointments. Writing your workouts into your calendar will make your more likely to follow through with them. By scheduling them for a specific time you be less likely to book conflicting appointments. Many people find it works best to schedule their walks for the whole week on Sunday evening. If you wait to walk until you can "find the time" you probably won't ever come across it.

Walk an Errand. Studies have shown that people who exercise to achieve an immediate and necessary goal are more consistent and stick with their plans longer then those who simply have a long-term health or fitness goal. See if you can figure out ways to cross things off your to-do list while walking. Can you walk to the store or the post office at lunch? Walking while taking care of tasks like these will give you an immediate sense of accomplishment.

Hit the Trail. Another way to vary your walking route is to take a hike. Being closer to nature always seems to make walks more enjoyable. Be sure you can already comfortably walk the distance for the hike you choose. Unstable terrain and abrupt inclines and declines make hiking that same amount of miles more difficult on the trail.

Tracking Your Workouts

One of the best ways to see how far you've come is to track your workouts. I have included a sample walking log at the end of the book, but you can make your log as simple or complex as you wish. (Don't get too complex though, or it will be become a chore to fill out.)

Some people like to keep a special notebook dedicated to tracking their walks, while others just like to jot a note about their walking time or distance in their daily calendar. The important thing is to have your log accessible, so you actually use it. Try keeping it by the phone or in the kitchen or in some other place that you'll see it daily and be prompted to record your workout.

Over time you can use your log as a tool to see what works and what doesn't. If you include comments about how you felt during your workout you can look back and see your progress. That 20-minute walk that was difficult when you started your program might be a breeze eight weeks later. You can also keep a running tally of your mileage, which can get to be a quite impressive number over the course of a year.

Rewarding Yourself

Rewarding yourself for reaching your goals is an important part of any walking plan. The rewards don't have to involve a lot of money, but they do have to be something you desire. The reward should also be appropriate for the goal. A short-term goal might have a small reward, while an important long-term goal might have a whopper of a prize at the end.

Short-Term Goal Rewards. Some ideas for short-term goal rewards include walking socks, shorts, and shirts; pedometers; fanny packs; or magazine subscriptions. Non-walking related rewards like a trip to the movies, a new CD, a manicure, a pedicure, or a pretty box of stationary are also nice. I don't recommend using meals out as a reward, simply because it sets you up for a potentially weird relationship with food. You can even reward yourself with indulgences that don't cost anything like a long bubble bath or an hour with a book you've wanted to read.

Long-Term Goal Rewards. Some ideas for long-term goal rewards are more expensive gear, like a waterproof jacket or pants; a new fleece; a heart-rate monitor; or a hydration pack. Non-walking related ideas include a massage or visit to a spa, a dance class, or even planning a vacation around a walking event.

5. Walking Techniques

You walk every day and have done so since you were an infant - why do you need to read a chapter on walking technique? There are lots of reasons actually. Certain techniques and form will help you walk fast enough to reap real fitness gains. That type of walking is called power walking. When you walk faster, your whole body, including your heart, is working harder. This leads to burning more calories and strengthening muscles.

Another benefit of using proper walking form is that it is more efficient than your normal, everyday-around-the-house walking. You'll be able to cover more ground using correct technique. The last, and most important reason, is that using proper walking form will decrease your risk of injury.

None of the techniques described below are difficult to master, but it does take some time to incorporate these changes into your walking form. Don't try to make all of the changes at once. It's a good idea to work on one piece at a time before you try to put it all together. You can focus on your stride for one walk, your torso for another, arms for another, etc.

LOWER BODY
Stride Length

The first thing that most walkers do when they try to walk faster is take bigger steps. That's probably the most common mistake beginners make. If you overstride, you will throw your body out of alignment, which is inefficient and could lead to injury.

The good news is that it's easy to correct. Every person's stride length is different. Keep that in mind if you walk with others, especially if they are much taller or shorter than you are. You need to walk at the stride length that's right for your body, not match somebody else's.

Here's an exercise to help you find your ideal stride length. Walk for about thirty seconds with your current walking stride. If you feel like you are reaching with your front leg, or if your head is bobbing up and down, your stride is probably too long. Bring it in a few inches and see how that feels. Keep bringing your stride length in until your steps start to feel cramped and hurried. Then slowly bring the length back out again. When you start to feel like you are reaching or if your head bobs, bring it back in. Keep fine tuning your stride length until it feels smooth and comfortable, neither exaggerated nor bunched.

Once you've got your stride length set, you can vary your walking speed by taking quicker, not longer, steps.

Stride Width

As silly as it sounds, stride width can make a huge difference in the efficiency of your walking form. An easy way to determine proper stride width is to find somewhere you can walk along a line painted in the road. (Please don't do this if there is any traffic around - you can just imagine the stripe instead.) Walk so that your feet fall just to each side of the stripe, almost as if you are walking along a balance beam. That's the width you want to develop for your stride.

Feet

The thing that makes walking different from running is that one foot is on the ground at all times. Your front foot should hit the ground heel first with your ankle flexed towards your body. Your foot should then roll along the ground in a smooth heel-to-toe motion as you step forward. When you begin to push off the toes of your back foot, the heel of your front foot should be hitting the ground.

After that becomes comfortable you'll want to focus on the big toe of your back foot. Think of pushing off with that toe as your foot leaves the ground to give your step a little more punch.

Hips

You may have seen race-walkers on TV and think that an exaggerated hip swing is the key to walking fast. Well, it's not. Your hips will swing naturally as a result of a tight stride width, not because you are thinking about swinging your hips. In fact, this is one part of your body that you won't have to think about at all when you walk. If you just walk along both sides of that imaginary stripe your hips will be doing exactly what they should.

UPPER BODY

Head. Your head should be in a neutral position, looking neither up nor down. You can check this alignment by noticing your chin...it should be parallel to the ground. Keeping your eyes focused about 20 to 30 feet in front of you, instead of down at your toes, will help you keep your head in the right place.

Shoulders. Your shoulders should be back and down away from your ears, but not uncomfortably so. Imagine a string pulling your chest up and out as you roll your shoulders back. Check in every once in a while to make sure you haven't started to hunch or shrug your shoulders as you get tired.

If you have ever been to a yoga class, you'll be familiar with mountain pose. That is the form your upper body should take. Your ears, neck and shoulders are all in a straight line.

Arms and Hands. I consider arms the secret weapon in going from strolling to power walking. It's amazing how you can use your arms to help propel you along. Your elbows should stay bent at a 90-degree angle throughout your walk. As you stride, your arms will swing along a plane parallel to your body. Your arms should be in close to your body, almost brushing your hips with each step. Your legs will follow the pace set by your arms. If you want to walk faster, all you have to do is concentrate on moving your arms faster. It's really quite amazing.

Just like your stride length, your arm movements should not be exaggerated. Your hands should stay within a relatively tight zone. Check that the hand in front comes up no higher than your chin and that the hand in back goes back no further than your hip.

How you hold your hands is important as well. They should be in relaxed rather than tightly clinched fists. I have a friend who says that she imagines holding a tortilla chip between her thumb and fingers. Her goal is keep her hands firm enough that the chip wouldn't fall out, but relaxed enough so the chip wouldn't break.

You might feel a little self-conscious at first walking with your arms bent. I know I did. All it took was a few sessions however and I was hooked - I walked faster and my rings still fit at the end of my walks. (One the added benefits of walking with your arms bent is that your fingers don't get swollen like they do when you walk with your arms straight.)

Keep in mind that your arms might get tired if you're not used to walking like this. You may want to alternative walking a few minutes with bent arms and then a few with straight arms until you're accustomed to it.

ARMS CONTROL

Your arms can really help you along, but you've got to control their movements. Try to avoid the following common sights I've seen on walking paths around the world:

The Flappers: These people swing their arms from side-to-side instead of forward-to-back, which looks like a flapper dance step. This side-to-side arm swing causes the upper body to work in the opposite plane as the lower body, completely throwing off any forward momentum.

The Mega Pumpers: Some walkers make huge, swinging arm pumps with every step. They bring their hands way up in front of their faces every time they swing their arms, as if they are trying to hit a punching bag in the sky. This exaggerated motion gives them upward, not forward, momentum.

The Marching Soldiers: These walkers swing their arms stiff and straight by their sides. Not only does this slow them down, it also leads to swollen hands at the end of their walk.

6. Preventing Injuries

Warm-up

It's important to incorporate a proper warm-up into your walking routine. If you'll just take a few minutes each walk to prepare your body for the task ahead, you'll reduce your risk of injury to joints and muscles. A proper warm-up releases sinovial fluid, a lubricant, into your joints. This will make them less creaky. A warm-up will also develop heat in your muscles, which will make them less likely to tear.

Easy Walk

Many people make the mistake of trying to stretch cold muscles. It's important to walk at an easy pace for about five minutes before beginning your stretches.

Stretches

After you've walked for five minutes, perform one set of each of the following stretches. These warm-up stretches are designed to take your different body parts through their range of motion. When stretching, always use slow, controlled moves, never bounce. Coordinate every movement with a deep inhale or exhale, being careful not to hold your breath. As you move into a stretch, be sure that you don't stretch to a point that you feel pain. You'll want to feel a mild sensation of stretching, but it should not be uncomfortable in any way.

Ankle Flexion, Extension and Circles. Stand with your feet about shoulder width apart. Holding on to a rail or bench, so you don't lose your balance, slowly bend your right knee, bringing your right foot about six inches off the ground.

Inhale, and with an exhale, slowly point your toes toward the ground. Inhale as you flex your foot back towards your body. Repeat this about ten times.

Next, roll your ankle around in a smooth motion, as if your toes were making their way in a circle around the face of a clock. Repeat this five times before making five circles in the opposite direction.

Repeat with left leg.

Leg Swing. Stand with your feet about shoulder width apart. Holding on to a rail or bench, so you don't lose your balance, slowly bend your right knee and bring your thigh up parallel to the ground.

Swing your leg down and back, so that your bent knee goes past your standing leg like a pendulum, and then swing the leg forward again. Repeat this fifteen times, swinging your leg forward and back to prepare your hip for your walk.

Make sure not to take your leg back so far that you hyperextend your back.

Repeat with other leg.

Side Stretch. Stand with your feet about shoulder width apart, arms at your sides. Raise your left arm until it is straight over your left shoulder. Inhale, and with an exhale, extend your right arm down the side of your right leg, creating a stretch in your left side. As you inhale, come back up to standing.

Repeat five times on right side, and then switch to left.

Shoulder rolls. Stand with your feet about shoulder width apart, arms at your sides. With an inhale, shrug your shoulders up towards your ears, and as you exhale, roll your shoulders back and down.

Repeat five times and then change directions.

Cool Down

It's also important to take time to cool down after you complete your walk. This will help you get your heartbeat back down to its resting rate in a controlled manner. It will also prevent the pooling of blood in your extremities. Lastly, a proper cool down will jump start your body in the repair process that is necessary after exercise.

Easy Walk

Take the last five minutes of your walk to get your heart rate down closer to its resting level. Step slowly and take deep breathes as you walk. Only after you've finished your easy walk cool down should you move-on to the following stretches.

Stretches

After you've walked your muscles are warm and loose, so this is an excellent time to stretch for increased flexibility. You'll want to hold each stretch for 20 to 30 seconds. Again, it's important to use slow, controlled movements and never bounce in these stretches. If you feel any pain what so ever, ease back until you just feel a mild tension on the muscle.

Quadriceps/Hip Flexor Stretch. Stand with your feet about shoulder width apart. Holding on to a rail or bench, so you don't lose your balance, bend your right knee so that you can grab your right ankle and slowly bring it in close to your right buttocks.

Bring your ankle in until you feel a stretch in the front of your right leg. Take deep breathes and hold the stretch for 20-30 seconds.

Staying in the same position, focus on pushing your right hip forward and down. When you feel the stretch in the front of your hip, take deep breathes and hold for 20-30 seconds.

Repeat with other leg.

Calf Stretch. Stand facing a wall or tree. Take a step forward with your left leg, leaving your right leg straight behind you. Place your arms against the wall or tree and lean forward until you feel the stretch in the back of your straight right leg. Take deep breathes and hold the stretch for 20-30 seconds.

Staying in the same position, slowly bend your right knee so that you feel the stretch in your Achilles and shin. Again, take deep breathes and hold the stretch for 20-30 seconds.

Repeat with other leg.

Hamstring Stretch. Stand with your feet about shoulder width apart. Inhale, and when you exhale, slowly hinge forward from the hips until you feel a stretch in the back of your legs. Try to keep your back straight, even if that means using your hands on the front of the thighs to prop yourself up. Make sure that your head is not tilted back or forward, but rather that your neck is in line with your spine.

Take deep breathes and hold the stretch for 20-30 seconds.

Lower Back Stretch. Lie on your back. Bend your right knee and bring it in towards your chest by holding your upper shin. (Be careful not to grab your knee.) Contract the muscles of your left leg while your hold your right knee to your chest.

Take deep breathes and hold the stretch for 20-30 seconds.

Repeat with other leg.

THE HAZARDS OF WALKING WITH WEIGHTS

While you might be tempted to walk with hand or ankle weights, I advise against it. You will raise your heartbeat only slightly, not add much strength, and make yourself vulnerable to a host of injuries. Walking with weights can cause an increase in blood pressure as well as put undue strain on your joints.

If you want to build strength, you should do that through resistance training. If you want a harder walking workout, you can walk faster, walk more often, walk longer, or walk hills.

Weather Precautions

Walking in extreme temperatures, either hot or cold, takes some extra care on your part.

Walking in Hot Weather

In addition to the special clothing requirements I mentioned in the Getting Started chapter (light weight, light colored, loose fitting clothing and a wide-brimmed hat), walking in hot weather has other rules.

Stay Hydrated

If you wait to drink until you are thirsty, it's too late. For most people, water is absolutely the best thing to drink to hydrate yourself. A sports drink is really not necessary if you are exercising for an hour or less. Here are some rules for fluid intake during warm and hot weather:

Drink up to 32 oz of fluid in the two-hour period before you walk, including 8 oz of water about 15 minutes before you begin. (8 oz of water is equivalent to 1 cup of water.)

Drink 8 oz of water every 20 to 30 minutes while you're walking, even if you're not thirsty. This will help replace the water you lose when you sweat.

Drink up to 32 oz of fluid in the two-hour period after you walk, including 8 oz of water after you finish your cool-down and stretching.

If you're a person who sweats a lot, drink even more. You want drink enough water so that your urine is clear and plentiful.

Heat Smarts

If you can manage it, try to walk during the cooler times of the day. This will reduce your risk of heat-related illness or complications. Especially avoid the hours from 10am to 4pm if it is over 80 degrees.

Take it easy if the humidity is above 75%. Your body is cooled by the evaporation of sweat from your skin. If it's especially humid, the sweat does not evaporate, meaning that your body cannot cool down.

Wear waterproof sunscreen with a minimum of SPF 15 protection. Apply it generously about 20 minutes before your walk.

Wear sunglasses.

It takes about 10-14 days to acclimatize to hot weather. If you travel to a hot environment, cut your normal walking time in half for the first five days. Over the next five days you can gradually increase your walking time to its normal level.

Make concessions to the heat. Remember, serious health risks like heat exhaustion, dehydration and heat stroke are real possibilities if you push yourself too hard during hot and humid conditions.

If you ever feel dizzy, nauseated or weak while walking during warm or hot weather, move immediately to a cooler environment (inside or to a shady area) and lie down to decrease your chances of fainting. Drink a cold sports drink to replenish electrolytes.

Walking in Cold Weather

As I discuss in the Get Started chapter, special clothing is needed to walk safely in cold weather. The proper laying of this clothing is especially important, as is wearing a hat. Make sure that the layer against your skin, the "wicking layer" is a synthetic, non-cotton fabric that draws sweat away from your body. Depending on the temperature, you may need a warming layer between your wicking layer and your outer, wind resistant, layer.

It's imperative to take layers on and off as you warm up and cool down. You never want to sweat excessively during cold weather activity. If you find that you are sweating profusely, you are overdressed. You also don't want to be shivering. Use your layers to regulate your temperature.

Cold Smarts

As with hot weather, it's important to give yourself time to acclimatize to cold weather. Take it easy the first couple of days and then gradually increase your walking time.

Stay hydrated. Drink plenty of water before, during, and after exercise.

Be aware of the wind chill. Make sure that you don't have any skin exposed to the air if the wind chill is less than freezing.

Listen to Your Body

Perhaps the most important safety precaution you can take is to listen to your body. If you're shivering, your body is telling you to put on more clothes. If it's hot outside and you're sweating excessively, your body is telling you to take it easy. If you're sore and tired, your body might be telling you to take a day off. You just have to be willing to listen to what your body is trying to say.

Here are some things you can do to keep your body happy:

Make sure to warm up and cool down properly every time you walk.

Walk with proper technique and good shoes.

If you have an especially hard workout one day, alternate that with an easy workout the next.

Use Cross Training and Activity Days to vary your workouts and prevent overuse of certain muscles.

Take a day off if you feel especially sore, tired or find yourself with a lowered resistance to colds or headaches.

Walker Safety

Even though walking is good for you, there are some dangers of which you need to be aware. Taking a few precautions can ensure your safety.

Walking on Streets

If you walk on streets, that means you share the road with cars. Because cars are a lot bigger and faster than you, "sharing" in this case means that they basically own the street. It's up to you to be alert and do what you can to stay out of their way.

Try to walk on streets that have a sidewalk or that don't have much traffic. In general, you should walk so that you are facing on-coming traffic. That way you can see the cars coming and get out of their way. Obviously, if there is a blind corner or a busy street to cross on one side of the street and not the other, you should choose the safer side.

If you have to walk when it's dark outside, or during dusk or dawn, I highly suggest wearing a reflective safety vest and/or a blinking light. (See the Getting Started chapter.) You should also wear light colored clothing and walk on well-lit streets.

Walking on Tracks or Trails

If you walk on a trail or track you're lucky not to have to worry about cars. If you walk on a track, most tracks have the rule that walkers take the inside lanes and runners the outside ones. Try to stick with that rule or you might find yourself colliding with a runner.

On walking trails, depending on the surface, you may have to pay a little more attention to your footing. If there are rocks or roots in the path, be sure to step carefully. Sometimes urban multi-use paths are filled with bikers, skaters, runners and walkers. If you are going to "change lanes," take a look over your shoulder before you move to check that there are no bikers or skaters tearing up the path behind you.

Walking on a Slanted Surface

Whether it's the beach, the shoulder of a road, or a trail, you want to make sure that the surface you walk on is not overly slanted. This can cause muscle imbalance and injury. Try to find an even surface for your walks.

Personal Safety

I'll cover this subject in more detail in the Issues for Women chapter, but there are certain precautions that walkers of both sexes need to take. The most important thing is to let somebody know where you're going to walk and how long you expect to be gone. You might even want to consider walking with a cell phone in case you run into any problems. You should always be alert and aware of your surroundings. If someone seems suspicious or something just doesn't feel right, walk away immediately.

Dealing with Injuries

Sometimes even the most careful walkers will find themselves with an injury. Over-doing it one day may result in shin splints the next; a step on an uneven surface may lead to a sprained ankle; or an improper warm-up may lead to a pulled muscle.

It's important to recognize the signs of injury. Swelling, bruising, tenderness, pain during movement, and local fever are all signals that you've hurt yourself. Do not continue your regular workouts if you have any of these signs. Depending on the severity of your injury, you may

THE DREADED SHIN SPLINTS

Shin splints are a common walker malady. "Shin splints" is actually a catchall term for any pain in the shin area. An imbalance between a tight, strong calf muscle and weak shin muscles is a common cause. There are a number of ways to avoid shin splints. Walking on soft surfaces helps, as does stretching the calf and strengthening the shin. You can exercise the shin area by walking around on your heels or writing an imaginary alphabet with your toes while seated. Proper fitting shoes are important, as is making sure you never increase your mileage more than 10% in a week.

If you end up suffering from shin splints, you should ice the area and take a couple of days off from walking. You can swim or bike instead and then slowly start back with your walking.

want to go to the doctor or you might choose to take a few days off to see if that helps. See a doctor immediately if you experience severe pain or numbness, loss of movement in a joint, or have an infection, pus, or red streaks coming from an injury. You should also see a doctor for any injury that doesn't heal or improve in two or three weeks.

If you do find yourself with an injury, it's important to give your body time to recover properly. Your doctor will tell you the recommended amount of time to wait before resuming activity, but keep in mind that you need to have full range of motion and strength before jumping back into your regular workout schedule.

7. Starter Plan

The goal of the **Starter Plan** is to get you to a level where you can move on to the Improved Health Plan. The Starter Plan assumes that you have not been exercising at all previously. You'll begin slowly and then, over the course of six weeks, build a walking foundation.

Precautions

I mentioned this before, but it's so important that I'm going to say it again. Take care not to push yourself too hard at the beginning. Don't just jump in and try to start walking 20 minutes a day. By starting slowly and following the plan, you'll avoid getting burned out, overly sore, or even injured. Because your body isn't used to any physical activity, you've got to give it time to adjust to the new demands that you'll be placing on it.

Create a Habit

The most important aspect of this plan is that you create a walking habit. How far you walk is not nearly as important as the fact that you get out there and walk almost every day. Walking ten minutes every day will go a lot further towards developing a routine than walking 30 minutes twice a week. It takes effort to create a habit and it also takes effort to get your body in shape. Each of us only has a limited amount of energy. It is much more important for you to direct yours towards developing the daily habit of walking than to focus your efforts on covering long distances. You'll be wrestling with your willpower to get out the door every day, so give yourself a break and make your walking time short.

If you miss a day don't let that derail you. All you have to do is jump right back into the plan where you left off.

Movement Day

This plan designates one day a week a "Movement Day." You have lots of options on this day. You can walk, if you choose, or you can substitute some other activity for your walk. The only catch is that the activity has to be something that gets you moving.

There are tons of alternatives for this day. Think about ways that you can add activity to your life — You can take the stairs instead of the elevator. Use a basket at the grocery store instead of a cart. Stand up and pace while you are talking on the phone instead of sitting at your desk. Go dancing. Work in your garden. Play with your kids, grandkids, or dog. Clean the floors or wash windows. Walk instead of taking the tram at the airport. Once you start looking for opportunities to be active, they will show up everywhere!

This would be a good day to wear a pedometer if you have one to see how many steps you can take trying to incorporate more movement into your day. (See the Weight Loss Plan for more information on using a pedometer.)

Pace

It's important to walk at a pace that you can sustain for the duration of your workout. If you start to pant and feel out of breath, you are walking too fast. During the course of this plan, you should walk at a comfortable pace that would allow you to sustain a conversation with somebody.

STARTER PLAN – FIRST THREE WEEKS

	Su	M	T	W	Th	F	S
Week One	10 min – Focus on Stride Length	Movement Day – 10 min	10 min Focus on Stride Length	10 min Focus on Stride Length	10 min Focus on Stride Length	10 min Focus on Stride Length	10 min Focus on Stride Length
Week Two	10 min – Focus on head/shoulders	Movement Day – 10 min	10 min Focus on head/shoulders	10 min Focus on head/shoulders	10 min Focus on head/shoulders	10 min Focus on head/shoulders	10 min Focus on head/shoulders
Week Three	15 min – Focus on arm swing	Movement Day – 15 min	15 min Focus on arm swing	15 min Focus on arm swing	15 min Focus on arm swing	15 min Focus on arm swing	15 min Focus on arm swing

LEAN ON ME

If you're overweight and find that your joints hurt when you walk, you might want to consider investing in walking poles. Poles will help spread some of the impact of each step away from your knees and ankles and into your arms. As an added benefit, walking with poles burns more calories than walking without them. (See the Get Started chapter for more information on walking poles.)

Form

Just because you *could* sustain a conversation, however, doesn't mean you *should*. Even if you're walking with a buddy, I encourage you to spend some time each workout focusing on a different aspect of proper walking technique. Put the chitchat on hold for a few minutes and focus on your form. Review the chapter on Walking Technique each week to remind yourself what you should be thinking about when you focus on the different components of your form.

Warm-up and Cool-down

Don't forget to include the warm-up and cool-down that I outline in the Preventing Injuries chapter before and after each one of your workouts.

Reward Yourself

Try to set weekly goals for yourself. An appropriate goal might be to follow the plan workout at least six days a week. Another goal might be to walk for a minimum of ten minutes a day, even if you don't feel like it. If you reach your goals, reward yourself every couple of weeks. You deserve it.

STARTER PLAN – WEEKS FOUR THROUGH SIX

	Su	M	T	W	Th	F	S
Week Four	15 min – Focus on feet	Movement Day – 15 min	15 min Focus on feet	15 min Focus on feet	15 min Focus on feet	15 min Focus on feet	15 min Focus on feet
Week Five	20 min – Focus on stride width	Movement Day – 20 min	20 min Focus on stride width	20 min Focus on stride width	20 min Focus on stride width	20 min Focus on stride width	20 min Focus on stride width
Week Six	20 min – Focus on stride length and arm swing	Movement Day – 20 min	20 min Focus on stride length and arm swing	20 min Focus on stride length and arm swing	20 min Focus on stride length and arm swing	20 min Focus on stride length and arm swing	20 min Focus on stride length and arm swing

After Week Six

Way to go! Making it through six weeks is a big accomplishment. If you feel comfortable doing the 20-minute walk, you can now move to the Walking for Improved Health plan. If making it for 20-minutes still feels like an effort, take a few more weeks at this level before moving to the next plan.

8. Improved Health Plan

Many people are motivated to start a walking program because they want to improve their health. Some may get some bad news about their cholesterol levels or blood pressure during a visit to the doctor's office. Others might have a family history of disease that they want to try to fend off. Whatever the reason, the good news is that developing a regular walking habit is a proven way to lower your risk of many diseases.

Precautions

This plan assumes that you have either worked your way through the Starter Plan, or that you are already fit enough to walk twenty minutes a day. If you have any question about your fitness level, I encourage you to begin with the Starter Plan before launching into the Improved Health Plan. Doing so will help you avoid burnout and injury.

Taking It from the Top

This plan has been developed from a statement made by three organizations that can be considered experts when it comes to the health of all Americans. The Surgeon General, the Center for Disease Control, and the American College of Sports Medicine have all made the following recommendation concerning physical activity: *Every U.S. adult should accumulate 30 minutes or more of moderate-intensity physical activity on most, preferably all, days of the week.* This simple sentence is sufficient to provide the outline for the Improved Health Plan.

Accumulate 30 Minutes or More

The good news is the word "accumulate." This means that your total minutes of activity can be spread out over two or even three walking sessions per day and you can still derive health benefits. If 30 minutes seems like a daunting number, take heart in the fact that you can break it down into fifteen or even ten-minute chunks. Even if your schedule is packed to the bulging point, certainly you can find ten minutes three times a day to walk.

Many people make the mistake of saying, "Oh, I only have 10 minutes to walk right now, it's not even worth it." That is absolutely not the case. You don't have to wait until you have a free half hour. Go walk those ten minutes now and get them out of the way. You'll feel better for it and make progress towards your 30-minute total.

According to the experts, 30 accumulated minutes per day is the minimum time needed to see the health benefits associated with regular physical activity. Notice the words "or more." These experts are also saying that accumulating more than 30 minutes of activity is desirable. The goal of this plan is to get you up to 45 minutes of walking per day.

Moderate-Intensity Physical Activity

Many people get confused about intensity levels when it comes to walking. They wonder how fast and hard they should be trying to go. "Moderate-intensity activity," when applied to walking, refers to a pace that will burn about 150 calories over thirty minutes of walking. Specifically, that translates to walking two miles total at a 15-minute mile pace.

The easiest way to calculate your walking pace is to find an area to walk where a mile is marked. That can be a local walking trail, the local school track, or even a mile measured out with your car. Try to find a flat course to time your one-mile walk. (If you're walking on a quarter-mile track, 4 laps in the inside lane is the equivalent of a mile.)

Do your stretches and begin your walk as usual. After warming up for about ten minutes, you will time your one-mile walk. Using a watch with a second hand, preferably one with a timer, walk the mile at your normal walking pace. Be sure to take time for a proper cool down afterwards. If you finished your mile in around 15 minutes, you are walking at moderate intensity. If you finish the mile in over 15 minutes, try to pick up your speed a little over the course of the next few weeks and then, after a month, measure your mile time again.

Remember, you increase your speed by making your **stride quicker, not longer.** If you try to speed up by increasing the length of your steps, you will be uncomfortable and might even end up injuring your back or knees.

Most, Preferably All, Days of the Week

That's right. Consistency is the key to walking your way to better health. Your real goal is to create a walking habit. As with the Starter Plan, how far you walk is not as important as the fact that you get out there and walk almost every day.

Habits aren't formed by random luck, but rather by repetition. It takes real work to develop a walking routine. Don't be tempted to substitute an hour-long walk three times a week for a daily 30-minute walk. At this point it is still more important for you to direct your energy towards developing the daily habit of walking than to focus your efforts on covering long distances. Only through repetition, day after day, will walking become an ingrained part of your life.

If you do have to miss a day or two, don't let that derail your plan. Just start back in where you left off and you'll soon be back on track.

A WALK A DAY HELPS KEEP THE DOCTOR AWAY
Developing a habit isn't the only reason to walk every day. New studies have shown that some of the benefits of exercise are triggered immediately after an exercise session rather than developed over time. A single walking session can have short-term positive effects on your levels of good cholesterol, blood pressure, and glucose control. You should try to exercise every day and minimize the number of days you miss to reap these short-term benefits.

Movement Day

Like the Starter Plan, this plan designates one day a week a "Movement Day." This gives you more options and helps you keep fresh. You can substitute any moderate intensity activity for walking on this day. I've designated Tuesday as movement day, but you can choose whichever day of the week works best with your schedule.

There are tons of alternatives for this day. Think about ways that you can add activity to your life → You can take the stairs instead of the elevator. Use a basket at the grocery store instead of a cart. Stand up and pace while you are talking on the phone instead of sitting at your desk. Go dancing. Work in your garden. Play with your kids, grandkids, or dog. Clean the floors or wash windows. Walk instead of taking the tram at the airport. Once you start looking for opportunities to be active, they will show up everywhere!

This would be a good day to wear a pedometer if you have one to see how many steps you can take trying to incorporate more movement

IMPROVED HEALTH PLAN – FIRST THREE WEEKS

	Su	M	T	W	Th	F	S
Week One	20 min – Focus on Proper Stride Length	20 min – Focus on Proper Stride Length	Movement Day – 20 min	20 min Focus on Proper Stride Length	20 min Focus on Proper Stride Length	20 min Focus on Proper Stride Length	20 min Focus on Proper Stride Length
Week Two	20 min – Include timed 1-mile walk	20 min – Focus on Proper head/shoulder positioning	Movement Day – 20 min	20 min Focus on Proper head/shoulder positioning	20 min Focus on Proper head/shoulder positioning	20 min Focus on Proper head/shoulder positioning	20 min Focus on Proper head/shoulder positioning
Week Three	25 min – Focus on Proper arm swing	25 min – Focus on Proper arm swing	25 min – Focus on Proper arm swing	25 min – Focus on Proper arm swing	25 min – Focus on Proper arm swing	25 min – Focus on Proper arm swing	25 min – Focus on Proper arm swing

into your day. (See the Weight Loss Plan for more information on using a pedometer.)

Pace

Don't overdo it when you try to increase your pace. Remember, you should not be walking so fast that you are panting or out of breath. Your **working pace** should be fast enough that you feel you are pushing yourself, but not so fast that you are out of breath.

Form

While you are developing the walking habit, it's important to make sure you're also in the habit of using proper form. Even if you walk with a friend, take some time during the first third of your workout to focus on your walking technique. Even a five-minute conversation break to focus on the component of your form outlined in the plan will help you integrate proper technique. Review the Walking Technique chapter at the beginning of every week to remind yourself what you should be thinking about as your focus on your form.

Warm-up and Cool-down

Don't forget to include the warm-up and cool-down that I outline in the Preventing Injuries chapter before and after each one of your workouts.

Mid-Plan Lag

It's not unusual for people's enthusiasm to falter after about six weeks. Be sure to reread the section about motivation in the Choosing Your Plan and Sticking With It chapter if you feel yourself starting to slip. Incorporating some of the strategies outlined there may be just the spark you need to relight that fire.

One of the reasons I start this plan on Sunday is that many people have more free time on their weekends. There's nothing like starting the week right by getting a walking session in before the chaos of the

(Continued on page 70)

IMPROVED HEALTH PLAN – WEEKS FOUR THROUGH SIX

	Su	M	T	W	Th	F	S
Week Four	25 min – Focus on Smooth Heel to Toe Motion	25 min – Focus on Smooth Heel to Toe Motion	Movement Day – 25 min	25 min Focus on Smooth Heel to Toe Motion	25 min Focus on Smooth Heel to Toe Motion	25 min Focus on Smooth Heel to Toe Motion	25 min Focus on Smooth Heel to Toe Motion
Week Five	30 min – Focus on Proper Stride Width	30 min – Focus on Proper Stride Width	Movement Day – 30 min	30 min Focus on Proper Stride Width	30 min Focus on Proper Stride Width	30 min Focus on Proper Stride Width	Take a 30 min. hike for a change of scenery
Week Six	30 min – Include a timed 1-mile walk	30 min – Focus on Proper Stride Length and arm swing	Movement Day – 30 min	30 min – Focus on Proper Stride Length and arm swing	30 min – Focus on Proper Stride Length and arm swing	30 min – Focus on Proper Stride Length and arm swing	30 min – Focus on Proper Stride Length and arm swing

IMPROVED HEALTH PLAN – WEEKS SEVEN THROUGH NINE

	Su	M	T	W	Th	F	S
Week Seven	35 min – Focus on Pushing Off With Big Toe	35 min – Focus on Pushing Off With Big Toe	Movement Day Focus on Pushing – 35 min	35 min Focus on Pushing Off With Big Toe	35 min Focus on Pushing Off With Big Toe	35 min Focus on Pushing Off With Big Toe	35 min Focus on Pushing Off With Big Toe
Week Eight	35 min – Focus on Proper head/shoulder positioning	35 min – Focus on Proper head/shoulder positioning	Movement Day Focus on Proper – 35 min	35 min Focus on Proper head/shoulder positioning	35 min Focus on Proper head/shoulder positioning	35 min Focus on Proper head/shoulder positioning	35 min Focus on Proper head/shoulder positioning
Week Nine	40 min – Focus on Quicker arm swing	40 min – Focus on Quicker arm swing	Movement Day Focus on Quicker – 40 min	40 min – Focus on Quicker arm swing	40 min – Focus on Quicker arm swing	40 min – Focus on Quicker arm swing	Take a 40 min. hike for a change of scenery

IMPROVED HEALTH PLAN – WEEKS TEN THROUGH TWELVE

	Su	M	T	W	Th	F	S
Week Ten	40 min – Include timed 1-mile walk	40 min – Focus on Slightly Decreasing Stride Width	Movement Day – 40 min	40 min Focus on Slightly Decreasing Stride Width	40 min Focus on Slightly Decreasing Stride Width	40 min Focus on Slightly Decreasing Stride Width	40 min Focus on Slightly Decreasing Stride Width
Week Eleven	45 min – Focus on Stride Length	45 min – Focus on Stride Length	Movement Day – 45 min	45 min Focus on Stride Length	45 min Focus on Stride Length	45 min Focus on Stride Length	45 min Focus on Stride Length
Week Twelve	45 min – Focus on Putting it all together	45 min – Focus on Putting it all together	Movement Day – 45 min	45 min – Focus on Putting it all together	45 min – Focus on Putting it all together	45 min – Focus on Putting it all together	45 min – Focus on Putting it all together

working week. Beginning the plan on Sunday helps assure that you get the week off to a good start, which can help keep you motivated.

After Week 12

First of all – Congratulations! Sticking to the plan for three months is quite an accomplishment. Be sure to reward yourself.

Once you have made your way through all twelve weeks of the improved health plan, you have a couple of options. Your first choice is to stick with this plan. Just keep repeating the week twelve workout, but focus each week on a different aspect of your walking technique. Another option is to move to the Walking for Fitness plan. It's up to you.

9. Improved Fitness Plan

Health vs. Fitness

The first question that many people ask is, "What's the difference between health and fitness?" For the purposes of this book, improved health is defined as lowering your risk of disease. That includes things like lower total cholesterol levels, decreased blood pressure, and lower stress levels.

Improved fitness, on the other hand, goes beyond that. It assumes lowering your risk of disease, but also includes improved cardiorespiratory performance. To improve your fitness level you must take a step beyond the previous plans. This is where you're really power walking. It's harder work, but the rewards are greater as well.

Precautions

Because this plan will involve stressing your heart to make it stronger, you want to make sure you have your physician's clearance. It also assumes that you are very comfortable walking 45-minutes a day at a moderate-intensity pace. If you have any doubts, I encourage you to begin with either the Starter or Improved Health Plan and work your way up to the Improved Fitness Plan. This will help prevent injury by making sure that you don't try too much too soon.

Getting a Baseline

Unless you know where you started, you won't know if you've made progress. Knowing where you are now in terms of fitness will also help you develop reasonable and attainable goals. You'll test your cardiorespiratory fitness by timing yourself in a one-mile walk. You'll want to do the test either on a flat walking trail that has one mile marked out, or at a school track that measures one quarter of a mile (where you'll do four laps in the inside lane.) Warm up and walk for five minutes at your normal pace before beginning the test.

For the test, you'll time yourself as you walk one mile as fast as you can. Obviously if you begin to feel light headed or start to breath too hard, you'll need to slow down or stop. After you finish your mile, continue walking slowly for five minutes to cool down.

After you get home, find your time on the following chart to determine your starting cardiorespiratory fitness level. Be sure to record your time and fitness rating in your walking log so that you can refer to it later.

Take the example of Linda, a 38-year old woman. She walked her baseline mile in 17:25. Looking at the chart below, that would place her in the "Average" category:

Fitness Category	Women under 40	Women over 40	Men under 40	Men over 40
Excellent	13:30 or less	14:30 or less	13:00 or less	14:00 or less
Good	13:31 – 16:00	14:31 - 17:00	13:01 - 15:30	14:01 – 16:30
Average	16:01 – 18:30	17:01 – 19:30	15:31 - 18:00	16:31 – 19:00
Below Avg.	18:31 – 20:00	19:31 – 22:00	18:01- 19:30	19:01 – 21:30
Low	20:01 or more	22:01 or more	19:31 or more	21:30 or more

Reprinted by permission of The StayWell Company, St. Paul, MN

Goal Setting

Once you have completed your timed 1-mile walk, you can use it as a starting point to set your goal. When setting your new goal time there are a few things you need to keep in mind. First, it's important to realize that it takes time, about 12 weeks, to improve your cardiorespiratory fitness level. So, make sure that you set your goal date three months out from today.

I recommend setting a goal time that is one minute and fifteen seconds faster than your baseline time. Your goal time should never exceed two minutes and thirty seconds faster than your baseline time. That just wouldn't be realistic. Remember, one of the important things about a goal is that it be reachable.

Using Linda as our example, you'll recall that she walked her baseline mile in 17:25, which fell into the "Average" category. Linda walked her baseline mile on June 1st. Linda's would like to take 1 minute and fifteen seconds off her baseline time, so her goal time is 16:10. Her goal date will be 12 weeks from June 1st, which is August 24th.

Determine your 1-mile walk goal based on your baseline walk time and write that down in your walking log. Be sure to remember to retest yourself in the 1-mile walk on that date.

Reaching Your Goal

There are many factors that will affect your ability to reach your goal. How often you walk, how hard you walk, how long you walk and how much rest you give your body will all have an impact. The following Improved Fitness Plan takes all those factors into account.

Measuring How Hard You're Working

Studies have shown that in order to make improvements in cardiorespiratory fitness, you have to push yourself harder than you have in the past. That can be done by walking more often, walking longer, or walking harder.

If you are starting the Improved Fitness Plan, you should already be able to comfortably walk 45 minutes per day, six days a week at your working pace. Remember that in the Improved Health Plan, we defined your working pace as fast enough that you feel you are pushing yourself, but not so fast that you are out of breath.

The Improved Fitness plan offers more specific guidelines for you to judge how hard you are working. There are two ways to determine your cardiorespiratory effort.

- The first method is the simplest. With it you don't have to make any calculations or buy any new equipment. (It's also for anybody on medicines, like Beta Blockers, that effect heart rate.) It is called the **Perceived Exertion Method**.

- The second method is for people who like precision. It involves making calculations and buying a heart rate monitor. That is the **Target Heart Rate Method**.

The plan is the same no matter which method you use to figure out how hard you are working. You know yourself better than anybody, so it's up to you to decide the method that you want to use to measure your walking intensity level. I will cover the Perceived Exertion Method here, but have included the same plan using the Target Heart Rate Method in the Appendix. Choose whichever method works best for you, your budget, and your personality.

Perceived Exertion Method

The beauty of the Perceived Exertion Method is its simplicity. As you are walking you will monitor your effort on a scale of one to ten. You will have a Perceived Exertion Target (usually between 4 and 7) and will try to stay at that effort level as you walk. See the definition of the different effort levels in the table below.

PERCEIVED EXERTION (PE) TABLE

0	No effort at all – standing still
1	Very low effort
2	Light effort
3	Moderate effort; you can walk and hold a conversation
4	
5	Working Effort; conversation requires some energy but is not difficult
6	
7	Very strong effort; conversation is difficult
8	
9	Extremely strong effort; conversation isn't in the picture
10	Maximum effort

Focus on Form

It's still important, even on the Improved Fitness Plan, to take five or ten minutes each walk to work on your form. For some people, poor form may be holding them back from increasing their walking speed. Read over the Walking Technique chapter at the beginning of each week so that you can remember what to think about as you focus on the different aspects of your form.

Movement Day

Like the Starter and Improved Health Plans, this plan designates one day a week a "Movement Day." This gives you more options and helps you keep fresh. You can substitute any moderate intensity activity for walking on this day. I've designated Tuesday as Movement Day, but you can choose whichever day of the week works best with your schedule.

There are tons of alternatives for this day. Think about ways that you can add activity to your life — You can take the stairs instead of the elevator. Use a basket at the grocery store instead of a cart. Stand up and pace while you are talking on the phone instead of sitting at your desk. Go dancing. Work in your garden. Play with your kids, grandkids, or dog. Clean the floors or wash windows. Walk instead of taking the tram at the airport. Once you start looking for opportunities to be active, they will show up everywhere!

This would be a good day to wear a pedometer if you have one to see how many steps you can take trying to incorporate more movement into your day. (See the Weight Loss Plan for more information on using a pedometer.)

Cross Training Day

Cross Training, which is basically participation in sports other than walking, will help balance out the use of your muscles, help prevent injury, and keep you fresh. See the chapter on Cross Training for more information about this day.

Enter a 5k or 10k

You'll notice that this plan includes walking two 5k or 10k races. Don't be intimidated by that. Races are a great way to keep your motivation level high and have fun to boot. You're surrounded by other active people, fans are cheering you along, and you feel a real sense of accomplishment at the end of the walk. Most cities have a newspaper that lists upcoming races and you can also search for them on the internet. You might want to enter a 10k in another town so that you combine your race with a weekend getaway. Don't worry about your target heart rate, your perceived exertion or your form...just go out and have a good time.

Here are some tips for your first race:

Enter a large race if possible. There are many benefits to having your first race be a large one. The bigger the race, the more walkers

THE RACE JITTERS

The first time I decided to walk a 10k I got to the starting line and almost didn't continue. It was small race and the vast majority of people there were runners. I just knew that I was going to be the last person on the course. I told my husband, a runner, not to wait at the finish line, because I didn't want him to see how much later I would come in behind everybody else. I felt horrible envisioning it.

Of course, in reality, things turned out much differently than I pictured. I walked a nice, steady pace and ended up passing many people along the way. I was far from the last person on the course, but even if I had been, the race staff and volunteers were all so nice, it just wouldn't have mattered. I enjoyed being around other people focused on the same goal and had fun at the post-race "party." My feelings of insecurity were valid, but they were also unnecessary.

there will be. A small race may only have a handful of walkers, where a large race, simply due to percentages, may have hundreds. That way you won't feel alone when the runners go zooming off ahead of you.

Another benefit is that there will be people around you the whole time you walk. That just makes it fun. Large races also generally have some sort of party or concert at the finish line, which helps you celebrate your accomplishment.

Walk with a friend. Walking with a friend means that you can train together and hold each other accountable. It also means that you'll have some moral support when you feel those starting line jitters. There's something about being with a buddy that helps dispel fears.

Stay away from "killer" races. Certain races have developed hellish reputations. They are either especially hilly or hot or a combination of both. Hold off on the "killers" until you've had a couple of successful race experiences. It's really important to have a nice time your first race. If you are entered in something called "The Hotter than Hell" or "The Toughest 10k", chances are it won't be that pleasant. It may be memorable, but not necessarily fun.

Don't Use New Equipment. Race day is not the time to wear anything that hasn't been tried and tested, be that shoes, socks, shorts, or shirts. Make sure that you've walked in all the gear you're using for your race. Shoes should be tested out for at least three weeks before racing in them.

Proper Rest

As you start to work your body harder, it's important to make sure it's getting the right amount of rest. If you are fatigued, you should take a day off, because it might mean that you are overtraining. Other signs of overtraining include unusual soreness, susceptibility to colds and headaches, depression or frustration, and dreading your workouts. If you have any of these signs you should take a good look at whether you have been ignoring your body's pleas for rest.

Warm-up and Cool-down

Don't forget to include the warm-up and cool-down that I outline in the Preventing Injuries chapter before and after each one of your workouts.

Interval Training

Once you have a strong base upon which to build (after week four), we will work on increasing your speed and improving your cardiorespiratory capacity through Interval Training. Interval Training means that you will increase your walking intensity for short periods of time during your workout. These bursts of speed get your metabolism burning as well as prevent plateaus.

IMPROVED FITNESS PLAN – BUILDING THE STRONG BASE

	Su	M	T	W	Th	F	S
Week One	Warm-up 1-mile Walk Baseline Test Cool-down	Walk 45 min PE = 7 Focus on Proper Stride Length	Movement Day – 45 min	Walk 45 min PE = 5 Focus on Proper Stride Length	Walk 45 min PE = 7 Focus on Proper Stride Length	Cross-Training Day Or Day Off	Walk 45 min PE = 5 Focus on Proper Stride Length
Week Two	Walk 45 min PE = 4 Focus on Proper head/shoulder positioning	Walk 45 min PE = 7	Movement Day – 45 min	Walk 45 min PE = 6 Focus on Proper head/shoulder positioning	Walk 45 min PE = 7	Cross-Training Day Or Day Off	Walk 55 min PE = 6/Focus on Proper head and shoulder positioning
Week Three	Walk 50 min PE = 4 Focus on Proper arm swing	Walk 50 min PE = 7	Movement Day – 50 min	Walk 50 min PE = 6 Focus on Proper arm swing	Walk 50 min PE = 7	Cross-Training Day Or Day Off	Enter 5- or 10-k Focus on fun
Week Four	Walk 50 min PE = 4 Focus on Smooth heel to toe motion	Walk 50 min PE = 7	Movement Day – 50 min	Walk 50 min PE = 6 Focus on Smooth heel to toe motion	Walk 50 min PE = 7 Focus on Smooth heel to toe motion	Cross-Training Day Or Day Off	Warm-up 1-mile timed walk – cool down Continue walking at moderate pace if you feel like it.

Note: "PE" means Perceived Exertion

In between intervals you will keep walking, but at a lower intensity. This is called recovery time.

Here's an example of an interval workout. In this workout you walk at a constant pace for 20 minutes, then do 5 two-minute intervals each followed by a two-minute recovery walk. After you finish the intervals you will return to 15 minutes of constant pace walking.

20 minutes at Perceived Exertion = 6
2 minutes at Perceived Exertion = 8 followed by
2 minutes at Perceived Exertion = 4
for a total of 20 minutes
15 minutes at Perceived Exertion = 6

Intervals and Hills

For the last month of the walking for fitness plan you will increase the intensity of your intervals and throw in some hill workouts as well. Find a gradually inclined hill or set of hills that takes you between two to four minutes to cover from top to bottom. Walking hills not only increases the workload on your heart, but it's also a form of resistance training for your legs because you are lifting the weight of your own body up an incline.

Here is the full workout:

20 minutes at Perceived Exertion = 6

Hill workout: Walk up hill at Perceived Exertion = 8; return and walk down hill at any comfortable pace. Repeat walking up and down hill for 25 minutes.

15 minutes at Perceived Exertion = 6

(Continued on page 85)

IMPROVED FITNESS PLAN –WEEKS FIVE AND SIX, INTERVAL TRAINING

	Su	M	T	W	Th	F	S
Week Five	Walk 55 min PE = 4 Focus on Proper Stride Width	20 min at PE = 6 2 min at PE = 8 followed by 2 min at PE = 4 for a total of 20 min 15 min at PE = 6	Movement Day 55 min	20 min at PE = 6 2 min at PE = 8 Focus on Proper followed by 2 min Stride Width at PE = 4 for a total of 20 min 15 min at PE = 6	Walk 55 min PE = 4	Cross-Training Day Or Day Off	Walk 65 min PE = 6 Focus on Proper Stride Width
Week Six	Walk 55 min PE = 4 Focus on Proper Stride Width	20 min at PE = 6 2 min at PE = 8 followed by 2 min at PE = 4 for a total of 20 min 15 min at PE = 6	Movement Day – 55 min	20 min at PE = 6 2 min at PE = 8 followed by 2 min at PE = 4 for a total of 20 min 15 min at PE = 6	Walk 55 min PE = 4	Cross-Training Day Or Day Off	Walk 65 min PE = 6 Focus on Proper Stride Width

IMPROVED FITNESS PLAN –WEEKS SEVEN AND EIGHT, INTERVAL TRAINING

	Su	M	T	W	Th	F	S
Week Seven	Walk 60 min PE = 4	20 min at PE = 6 2 min at PE = 8 followed by 2 min at PE = 4 for a total of 20 min 15 min at PE = 6 Focus on Proper Stride Length and arm swing	Movement Day 60 min	20 min at PE = 6 2 min at PE = 8 followed by 2 min at PE = 4 for a total of 20 min 15 min at PE = 6 Focus on Proper Stride Length and arm swing	Walk 60 min PE = 4	Cross-Training Day Or Day Off	Walk 70 min PE = 6 Focus on Proper Stride Length and arm swing
Week Eight	Walk 60 min PE = 4	20 min at PE = 6 2 min at PE = 8 followed by 2 min at PE = 4 for a total of 20 min 15 min at PE = 6 Focus on Pushing off with big toe	Movement Day – 60 min	20 min at PE = 6 2 min at PE = 8 followed by 2 min at PE = 4 for a total of 20 min 15 min at PE = 6 Focus on Pushing off with big toe	Walk 60 min PE = 4	Cross-Training Day Or Day Off PE = 4	Warm-up 1-mile timed walk/cool-down Continue walking at moderate pace for up to 30 min if you feel like it

IMPROVED FITNESS PLAN –WEEKS NINE AND TEN, HILL TRAINING

	Su	M	T	W	Th	F	S
Week Nine	Walk 60 min PE = 4 Focus on Proper head/shoulder positioning	Movement Day – 60 min	20 min at PE = 6 3 min at PE = 8 followed by 1 min at PE = 4 for a total of 24 min 15 min at PE = 6	Hill Workout	Walk 60 min PE = 4 Focus on Proper head/shoulder positioning	Cross-Training Day Or Day Off	Walk 70 min PE = 6 Focus on Proper head/shoulder positioning
Week Ten	Walk 60 min PE = 4 Focus on quicker arm swing	Movement Day – 60 min	20 min at PE = 6 3 min at PE = 8 followed by 1 min at PE = 4 for a total of 24 min 15 min at PE = 6	Hill Workout	Walk 60 min PE = 4 Focus on quicker arm swing	Cross-Training Day Or Day Off Focus on quicker arm swing	Enter 5- or 10-k Focus on fun

IMPROVED FITNESS PLAN –WEEKS ELEVEN AND TWELVE, HILL TRAINING

	Su	M	T	W	Th	F	S
Week Eleven	Walk 60 min PE = 4	20 min at PE = 6 3 min at PE = 8 followed by 1 min at PE = 4 for a total of 24 min 15 min at PE = 6	Movement Day – 60 min	Hill Workout PE = 4 Focus on Slightly Decreasing Stride Width	Walk 60 min Or Day Off Focus on Slightly Decreasing Stride Width	Cross-Training Day PE = 6	Walk 70 min PE = 6 Focus on Slightly Decreasing Stride Width
Week Twelve	Walk 60 min PE = 4	20 min at PE = 6 3 min at PE = 8 – 60 min	Movement Day	Hill Workout	Walk 60 min PE = 4 Focus on Your Total Form	Cross-Training Day Or Day Off Focus on Your Total Form	Warm-up 1-mile timed walk/cool-down Continue walking at moderate pace for up to 30 min if you feel like it

After Twelve Weeks

Congratulations. After completing this plan you should be feeling like one very strong walker. Be sure to compare your final 1-mile walk time with your initial 1-mile goal to see how you did. Once you finish this plan you can simply start over again at week one. That way your body will have a chance to rest and recover before you start your intervals and hills again. Be sure to set a new goal time for your 1-mile walk before you begin the plan again. (Remember, it's a valid goal just to want to maintain your current time, you don't always have to go faster and faster.)

A LEG UP ON RUNNERS

For some reason, a few of the walkers I know feel sheepish about not "graduating" to running. They shouldn't! Walking, much better on the joints that running, can actually be a harder workout as well. Because walking at high speeds doesn't depend on momentum as much as running does, walking fast can actually burn more calories than running at the same pace. The dividing line where walking starts to burn more calories than running at the same pace is about a 12-minute mile.

10. Cross Training

If you step back and take a look at the big picture, being healthy can be defined as the ability to live your day-to-day life with energy and vigor. That's the whole point isn't it? There are really three components to fitness that you need to cover in order to be healthy in that way. One of these components, cardiorespiratory fitness, you can attain through power walking. The other two components, strength and flexibility, are best improved away from the walking trail.

That's where cross training comes in. Cross training, participating in sports other than walking, allows you to develop muscles not used when walking. At the same time, it gives your walking muscles a chance to rest, so it helps prevent injuries. It will also keep you fresh mentally by adding variety to your routine.

There are many different types of cross-training activities. I have broken them down into three categories – resistance training, flexibility training, and cardiorespiratory training.

Resistance Training

Strength, one of the three components of fitness, can best be achieved through resistance training. While people traditionally think of weight lifting when they think of resistance training, there are other options as well. You can also use elastic bands, rubber tubing and Swiss balls to develop strength.

Strength training has a number of important benefits. One of the biggest benefits is that it helps maintain lean body mass. Studies have shown that as people age they lose 1/3 to 1/2 pound of muscle tissue per year. That can account for a 20 to 40% loss of muscle mass between the ages of 20 and 65.

Lean muscle burns more calories than other types of body tissue. When people lose muscle mass, they burn fewer calories on a daily basis, which almost inevitably leads to weight gain. This trend can be reversed through resistance training. By gaining lean muscle mass you can increase your resting metabolism, thereby burning more calories throughout the day (even when you are sleeping!).

Increasing the strength of your muscles will also improve muscle endurance. In addition, it can help prevent injuries, correct muscle

WOMEN AND THE BULKY MUSCLE MYTH

Many women are afraid to begin a resistance training program because they have a fear that they will turn out looking like Ms. Olympia. They don't want to have large muscles that will make them look "big." If you are one of these women, you really shouldn't worry.

Women's bodies respond differently to resistance training than men's do. Testosterone, which men have lots of, is the main source of bulky muscles. Women, with small amounts of this hormone, just don't bulk up naturally. In fact, most women who start a weight-training program go down a dress-size or two, not up.

imbalances, and just make it easier to carry out your daily tasks. Another important benefit of resistance training, especially for women, is that it helps lead to healthy bones.

When and Where to Resistance Train

Studies have shown that results can be achieved by lifting weights as little as one day a week, especially for beginners. Two or three strength workouts per week, once you're past that beginner stage, is optimal. It's important to separate all your resistance training sessions by at least one day, allowing your body to recover.

Resistance training can be done anywhere. I would advise those with little experience to join a gym where there are people who can teach safe and proper lifting techniques. A trainer can set up a personalized program as well as monitor your improvements and keep you accountable.

If joining a gym is not an option, you can also set up an adequate home gym by investing in rubber tubing, a Swiss ball, and some hand weights. Again, it would be good to work with a trainer at first so that you know you are doing the exercises safely. Many trainers will make housecalls.

Muscles to Work

The goal of your resistance training is to work the major muscles of your entire body. Again, a trainer can help you set up such a program. There are also many books and videos dedicated entirely to strength training.

Lower body exercises that you'll want to include will work your calves, shins, hamstrings, quadriceps, and gluts. These are obviously key muscles to be able to walk with speed and endurance. Your core stomach and back muscles are also very important to strengthen. They will help you maintain good walking form. Lastly, you want to work your shoulders, chest, biceps, and triceps. With a strong upper body you will be able maintain a rapid armswing, which leads to faster walking.

Flexibility Training

Flexibility, the third component of health, has long been overlooked. Only in the last few years have scientists come to understand the importance of flexibility training to overall wellness. Flexible muscles are much less prone to injury than tight ones. Loose muscles help you maintain fluidity and grace in your movements. Stretching also reduces muscle tension and, like strength training, helps prevent muscle imbalances.

There are a number of ways to increase your flexibility. One of those is through stretching. If you are the type of person who is disciplined enough to loosen your muscles groups with a stretching routine on your own, I congratulate you.

By "stretching routine" I mean much more than the stretches you do before and after each walking session. I mean taking the time two or three days a week to slowly stretch each muscle for 30 seconds, repeating each stretch three to five times. Remember, you want to make sure you don't ever bounce in any stretch and you should only stretch to a point of light tension, not pain.

If that sounds like something you can handle, you can should get a book or video on stretching and work your way through the muscles I outlined above in resistance training.

Many people however, just can't get themselves to stretch as much as they should. If you're one of those people, I highly recommend taking yoga. By committing yourself to yoga classes you will be stretching by coincidence. Instead of sitting there thinking about how boring stretching is, you'll be concentrating on the instructor's directions and moving yourself into different poses.

The great thing about yoga is that there are so many other benefits in addition to increased flexibility. Yoga also relieves stress, improves posture, strengthens your back, improves muscle tone, increases your breathing capacity, helps your circulation and builds better balance.

Some people are intimidated by the thought of entering a yoga class. Don't worry, you don't have to be able to tie yourself into knots to do yoga. There are a wide variety of poses that fit each person's needs based on physical condition and flexibility. Beginner classes start out with very simple poses that even people with extra-tight muscles can do.

YEAH, BUT WHAT ABOUT WEIRDOS?

Some people have the mistaken idea that yoga classes are filled with seed-eating, spaced out wackos. That's just not the case. Yoga, with all its amazing benefits, has moved into the mainstream. You're more likely to find busy executives and stressed out moms in yoga class than vacuous vagabonds.

Cardiorespiratory Training/Other Sports

Taking time to participate in other sports can keep both your mind and body fresh. I recommend doing something other than walking at least once a week. Some excellent low impact activities include biking, swimming, rowing, in-line skating, and cross-country skiing.

Swimming is one of my personal favorites because it is low impact and it works the upper body so effectively. It strikes a nice balance with walking, which is mainly a lower body sport. Bike riding is another good activity to balance with walking because it mainly works the quadriceps, while walking targets the hamstrings, calves and gluts.

Choose one of these activities, or any other sport you're interested in, and mix it with your walking routine.

Exercise Machines

If you are a member of a gym, another way to mix up your routine is to use the club's exercise machines. These are great options if temperatures are extreme or if rain is an issue. You can effectively cross train on stair steppers, elliptical trainers, stationary bikes, Nordic Traks, and rowing machines.

Gym classes are another nice cross training option. Now is a great time to check out the kickboxing or step class that you've always wanted to try. Spin class is another excellent cross training alternative. Gyms are constantly coming up with new classes to keep their

TREADMILL WALKING

Extremely hot or cold weather can make an indoor treadmill awfully inviting. There's no problem with doing your walking workouts on the treadmill. If you set the incline to a 1% grade, your effort will mimic walking on a flat surface outdoors. Because you're not dealing with outdoor elements, which allows you to walk faster than you would outside, it's good to pay attention to your perceived exertion level rather than the speedometer.

Your form is also important on the treadmill. While it's tempting to look down at all those displays and buttons, you should try to keep your chin parallel to the ground. Take care and pay special attention to your stride length as well, as people on treadmills have a tendency to overstride.

members entertained. Get the most out of your membership by giving each new class a try – who knows, you might find something you really like.

11. Nutrition

Good eating habits are a major component of healthy living. Exercise is very important, but you can undo much of the benefits you gain from walking with a poor diet. On the other hand, good nutrition habits can make a major difference not only in how you feel, but also in your overall wellness.

It's important to understand that this is a lifetime nutrition plan, NOT a diet. Many times when people diet they change their eating habits for a month or so, until they have lost some weight, but then they fall back into their old eating patterns. Because they have not made any lasting changes in how they eat, the weight slowly works it way back.

This plan is about making permanent changes in your eating habits. It's a plan for life – a long and healthy life.

Take It Slowly

In this chapter I'll outline twelve important changes you can make in your eating habits. Don't be overly ambitious and try to make all the changes at the same time. It will be too much. If you slowly integrate the changes into your life you'll be more likely to stick with them.

With that in mind, I recommend making no more than one change a week. Give yourself a little time to get used to the first change before you go rushing off to make the next one. Twelve weeks might seem like a long time, but remember, you're taking a lifelong view here. Three months is nothing when you compare it to the years you have yet to live.

Concentrate on the "Do's" – not the "Don'ts"

One of the problems that occurs when people diet is that they feel deprived. They forbid themselves to eat certain foods and then fantasize about those foods for weeks. Suddenly one day their willpower gives in (it always does eventually) and they find themselves binging on their fantasy food. The forbidden fruit is always the one we desire.

With that in mind, there are no forbidden foods with this plan. Nothing is banned, but quantities of the foods with low nutritional impact should be limited. That's the only way to make a lifetime change. Go ahead and have a cookie, or piece of chocolate, or beer, or piece of Brie. Just make sure that you savor one instead of pigging out on six.

Try to change your mindset concerning food. Instead of thinking about things you shouldn't eat, think of your meals in terms of all the

---

COOKIE MONSTER

I love cookies. I know that they are a food that I personally "need." Even if I feel a little heavy and am closely watching what I eat, I always indulge in a couple of really delicious, high quality cookies a week. (I do make sure they aren't the ones that are as big as Frisbees however.) It keeps me satisfied and prevents me from getting off track.

things you need to eat. It can actually be a fun challenge to figure out how to fit in all those fruits, vegetables and whole grains over the course of a single day. Healthy eating is influenced as much with what you DO eat as what you DON'T.

12 HABITS FOR LIFE
Week One - Eat Breakfast

A nutritious breakfast is fundamental. Eating breakfast is basically a signal to your body that you're not asleep anymore. It says, "Hey metabolism, I'm not lying in bed now, it's time to speed up." Breakfast is a great chance to sneak in a few fruit and vegetable servings as well. There are tons of options for quick, delicious and healthy breakfasts.

You want to make sure that your breakfast includes some low-fat protein, whole grains and at least one fruit or vegetable. Great morning protein sources include low fat yogurt, skim milk, low-fat cheese, egg whites, peanut butter or turkey. You can get your whole grains in the form of cereal, bread, tortillas, English muffins, waffles or bagels. (Make sure that they are made of whole-wheat flour, not enriched wheat or white flour) Tasty morning fruits and vegetables include berries, bananas, fruit juices, and tomatoes. There are many books, magazines and websites that list healthy breakfast menus if you need more ideas.

Non-breakfast eaters are often very resistant to starting their day with a meal. They have all sorts of excuses. One typical excuse is that they say they end up hungry before lunch when they eat breakfast. They probably do – and with good reason. If a person skips breakfast, his body stays in the slow metabolism "hibernation mode" until he wakes it up by eating lunch. If he were to start his day with a meal, he would boost his metabolism and get his body going right off the bat. Our bodies are designed to need fuel every 3-5 hours during the day. Three hours after breakfast, he might get hungry again. That's the perfect time for a healthy, mid-morning snack.

SPECIAL SMOOTHIES – MY FAVORITE BREAKFAST

A few years ago I had some jaw problems that temporarily prevented me from eating solid food. I started experimenting with the blender and came up with a breakfast concoction I've been eating ever since. This is the kind of smoothy that sticks to your ribs. I sometimes even eat it with a spoon. You get whole grains, dairy, fruit, protein, vitamins, and minerals all in one delicious package, and it tastes like a milkshake! Who says nutrition has to be boring?

Combine the following ingredients in a blender and enjoy:
- 1/2 cup frozen fruit (try strawberries, blueberries, peaches, mangos, melons...they are all delicious)
- 1/2 banana
- 2/3 cup whole grain cereal or 1/2 cup oatmeal (not instant)
- 1/2 cup low fat cottage cheese or low-fat, plain yogurt
- 1/3 cup skim milk
- 1/3 cup calcium fortified orange juice
- 1 tablespoon flax seed meal

People who don't eat breakfast usually end up eating large, calorie-laden lunches and dinners. It's much healthier to eat a nice breakfast and a reasonably sized lunch and dinner, along with a morning and afternoon snack, effectively spreading calorie consumption out over the course of the entire day.

Week Two - Switch to Low Fat and Skim Dairy Products

Dairy fat is saturated fat. That's the kind that's not good for you. By switching to skim (also known as "fat free"), and 1% dairy products, you'll eliminate some of the animal fats in your diet. Don't be fooled by 2% milk. The percentage in this case refers to the percentage of fat by weight, not by calories. A whooping 35% of the calories in "2% milk" come from fat.

Some people complain that skim milk is just too watery. If you feel that way, make the switch gradually. Go from 2% milk to 1% and then to skim over the course of a month or more. You'll be amazed, but after you start drinking skim for a while, whole or even 2% milk will clog your throat and seem as thick as cream.

Skim and low fat cottage cheese, milk, and yogurt taste can taste as good if not better than their full-fat counterparts. Cheese producers have also made great strides with their low fat cheeses. It used to be that low fat cheese tasted pretty much like cardboard. These days that's not the case. Experiment around and see which brands and types of cheeses you like best in their low fat versions.

Week Three - Eat a Variety of Colors

The National Cancer Institute recently launched a campaign called "Savor the Spectrum." The program is designed to get Americans thinking about eating a variety of fruits and vegetables. The best part of the plan is that it's so simple.

All you have to do is eat one or two serving of fruits or vegetables every day from each color group. By eating a variety of colors you are assuring yourself of a host of antioxidants. Antioxidants do things like prevent some cancers, stroke, heart attacks and diabetes. Intensely colorful fruits and vegetables also provide tons of vitamins, minerals and fiber. The more concentrated the color the better. That means putting dark green spinach on your sandwich instead of pale iceberg lettuce.

Here are the color groups and some examples of foods that fit the categories:

Yellow-Orange: carrots, oranges, tangerines, yellow bell peppers, mangos, grapefruit, summer squash, apricots, cantaloupe

- **Red**: tomatoes, strawberries, cherries, apples, red bell peppers, raspberries

- **Green**: spinach, arugula, asparagus, green beans, kiwis, broccoli, Brussels sprouts

- **Blue-Purple**: blueberries, plums, cabbage, raisins, beets, blackberries, eggplant

- **White**: onions, garlic

Week Four - Substitute Whole Grains for Refined Ones

You've probably read conflicting reports on carbohydrate consumption, which we can call The Great Carb Debate. Here's my take on it: Our bodies were designed to be fueled by carbohydrates and fats. Protein is supposed to be used as a building block, therefore it is not efficiently converted to fuel. We NEED carbohydrates. Having said that, there is no doubt that many people over-do it on the carbohydrate front. There is also no doubt that not all carbs are created equal.

Remember, there are "good carbs" and "bad carbs" as far as grains go. Good carbohydrates are made from whole, unrefined grains. They are nutritionally dense and calorically relatively light. These are the carbs you want to eat. Bad carbs, on the other hand, are highly refined, sugar-laden, and nutritionally weak. In addition, they are full of calories. It's important to substitute good carbs for bad.

You can tell if a carb is good by looking at the ingredients list on the package. The first item in a good carb will be "whole," not "refined" or "enriched." Whole grains are key. They keep you feeling fuller than refined grains, they have more fiber, and they also contain more vitamins and minerals. Be aware that many "wheat breads" are actually not made from whole grains. Be sure to check the ingredients list.

"Enriched wheat flour" is not the same thing as "whole wheat." You want whole wheat, not the enriched stuff.

Many bad carbs fall into what I call the White Flour Group. These are things like white bread, flour tortillas, most bagels, many pastas, white rice, sugar-laden cereal, and cookies. The good news is that you can find a whole grain version of almost everything in the White Flour Group. If you love bagels, you don't have to cut them out, you just have to find whole wheat ones. Same goes with pasta, tortillas, rice, cereal and even cookies. (Although you might have to make the whole grain cookies at home.)

Week Five - Emphasize the Sides

Americans, harking back to our robust farmer days, are accustomed to plates of food, especially dinner, with the protein dish as the main centerpiece surrounded by small sides of vegetables. We need to rethink that layout.

One of the easiest ways to make sure you're getting a balanced dinner is to imagine your plate divided into four quarters. Your protein serving should take up at most one of those quarters. Two other quarters should be filled with colorful vegetables, and the fourth with some type of whole grain. It may take some getting used to a first, but if you let your "side dishes" take more of a staring role, you'll be eating in much healthier proportions.

Week Six - Have a Restaurant Strategy

Many people tell me that they don't have any problem eating healthily at home, but when they step inside a restaurant it's another story. Often they end up eating as many calories in one meal as they normally do in an entire day. With most Americans eating out at least four times a week, that can really add up.

You need to have a specific strategy every time you walk into a restaurant. Restaurants are serving humongous portions of food these days. One strategy is to either share your entrée or ask the waiter to put half of it in a doggie bag in the kitchen before you are served. (I know from personal experience that if you try to use self-control to eat only half the food on your plate, you'll usually fail. If you have it put in the doggie bag from the get-go, you've got a lot better chance.) Another option is to order lunch size portions or appetizers for your main dish.

One friend of mine has the strategy of eating only what she orders. She doesn't touch the "free" tortilla chips or bread with olive oil that can turn a 600 calorie meal into a 1200 calorie one in the blink of an eye.

Also, don't be shy about asking the kitchen to prepare your meal in a special way. Most restaurants are used to customers asking for sauces to be left off or placed on the side, for fish or chicken to be broiled, not sautéed, or for any other healthy alternative you might come up with.

Another strategy of course is to eat out less often. Brown bagging your lunch can save you both money and calories. In addition, you can use the time you would have wasted getting to and from the restaurant and waiting for your food to take a nice mid-day walk.

PICKING FAST FOOD

There are times when you will be forced to go to a fast food restaurant. Don't worry, your nutrition plan is not necessarily blown for the day. Some restaurants, like Subway and Quiznos, offer healthy and tasty sandwiches and salads. You can get salads or grilled chicken at places like McDonalds and Burger King. Wendy's even has baked potatoes. Just limit or eliminate the mayonnaise, sour cream, creamy salad dressings, and salad oil.

Week Seven - Eat Fish At Least Twice a Week

Fish is one of those foods that packs a walloping nutritional punch. Not only is fish a great source of lean protein, even the fat on fish is healthy. Cold-water fish like salmon, mackerel and tuna are chock-full of a type of fat (omega 3) that protects against heart attacks. A recent study showed that people who ate fish 2-4 times a week cut their risk of heart disease by 30%.

Some people who haven't cooked fish before are intimidated about trying or think they will be put off by the smell. A fresh salmon fillet or tuna steak shouldn't have a "fishy" smell or taste and is as easy to prepare as a chicken breast. Grilling and broiling are two yummy and easy ways to prepare fish. Just be sure you don't cancel out the benefits of the fish by frying it or globbing it with tarter sauce.

Week Eight - Eat Heart-Healthy Fats

Not all fats were created equal and not all fats are bad for you. In fact, your body needs certain types of fat to process some vitamins, protect your internal organs, and to use as fuel. Some fats, like those found in fish, can even help protect against heart attacks.

The problem with the American diet is that most Americans eat lots of the kinds of fats that are bad for them. Which ones are they? Many unhealthy fats are solid at room temperature and come from animal sources. They include things like beef, pork, lard, butter, and other whole milk dairy products. Another type of "bad fat" can be found in margarine, fast food, and most processed snack foods. These bad fats are the kind that clog up your arteries and lead to heart disease.

The good fats come mainly from vegetable sources. They include olive, canola, corn and safflower oils as well as avocados and nuts. You need to make sure and work some of these into your diet every day. Good fats not only protect us against diseases, but they also keep us full and satisfied longer.

SPRAY IT ON

I don't know about you, but every time I try to pour just a little bit of olive oil out of the jar, I end up with far more oil in the pan than is necessary to cook my meal. Spray oils are a great solution. Pam, for example, makes a great olive oil spray. With the sprays I can lightly cover my cooking surface with oil instead of drowning it.

Now, the important thing is not to overdo it. Remember, a serving of nuts is just one ounce. That's a small handful, not five or six fists-full. One small handful of nuts per day is a good number to shoot for. You also want to limit your oil intake, even though it's the good kind, to 1-3 teaspoons daily.

Week Nine – Substitute Water/Juices for Alcohol/Soda

Soft drinks are a nutritional wasteland. A single Coke, for example, has an entire day's allowance of sugar and no vitamins or nutrients. Trying to cut back on your soda consumption can be hard, but it's not impossible. Even diet soft drinks, full of chemicals, are not good for you. If you're absolutely addicted to soft drinks however, the diet versions are preferable. Don't be fooled by "fruit flavored drinks" either. Most of them, even if they have added vitamin C, are primarily sugar.

Water is the best alternative. It has no calories and your body needs it to function properly. If you crave more flavor however, try mixing fruit juices with carbonated water for a nice soft drink substitution.

As far as alcohol goes, studies have shown that moderate consumption of alcohol can be beneficial as long as you don't have a health problem that can be made worse by alcohol. It's important to know the definition of "moderate" however. Alcohol consumption should be limited to a maximum of one drink a day for women and two for men. (That doesn't mean abstaining during the week and then having six drinks on Saturday night either. Binging drinking offers none of the protection from cardiovascular disease that moderate drinking can provide.)

Week Ten - Beans, Beans...(You Know the Rest)

Beans really are a magical fruit. Eating three or four servings of beans a week has been shown to lower blood pressure and reduce the risk of heart disease and cancer. Beans are also chock-full of fiber, which helps lower cholesterol and blood sugar. In addition, they are a great low fat source of protein, vitamins and minerals. Just made sure they are prepared in a healthy way without those bad fats. Lentils, chickpeas, and blackbeans are some of my favorites.

There are some steps you can take if you like beans, but they don't like you (so to speak.) Try adding them to your diet gradually, starting with just one or two servings per week. Soaking uncooked beans overnight before you prepare them and then changing the water can also help cut down on the gas factor.

Week Eleven - Try New Foods

Again, one of the keys to maintaining a healthy eating plan for life is to focus on all the wonderful things that are good for you. Experiment with new foods to add pizzazz to your diet. Tired of brown rice and whole what pasta? Try whole-wheat couscous, barley, or quinoa. Apples and oranges got you yawning? Sample some passion fruit or guava for a new flavor treat. Buy some of those weird looking squash you see at the grocery store in the fall and look up a recipe on the internet – it may turn out to be one of your new favorites.

Week Twelve - Learn Your Serving Sizes

Servings can be a tricky thing. You know that you need a certain amount of servings from each food group per day. The problem of course is that America is being super-sized. You hear that you need 7-

12 servings of whole grains per day and you imagine eating 7 bagels...hate to disappoint you, but one bagel constitutes about three servings.

Here are the recommended servings per day for each food group, and more importantly, what constitutes a serving size.

Whole Grains: 5-9 servings per day
- 1/2 cup cooked rice, pasta or cereal (about the size of a hockey puck)
- 1 oz cold cereal (usually about 2/3 to 1 cup)
- 1 slice bread (size of a cassette tape)
- 1 tortilla
- 1/2 a packaged bagel, English muffin, or small hamburger bun (hockey puck size)
- 1/3 a big bagel from the bagel store

Fruits and Vegetables: 5-9 servings per day
- 1 cup raw, leafy vegetables
- 1/2 cup other vegetables
- 1/2 large banana
- 1 medium fruit (apple, orange, grapefruit, pear, etc)
- 1/2 cup canned or frozen fruit
- 1/2 cup dried
- 6 oz fruit juice (about 3/4 cup)

Dairy: 2-3 servings per day
- 1 cup (8 oz) skim milk
- 1/2 cup calcium fortified OJ
- 1 oz cheese (about the size of a box of matches or 4 dice)
- 1 cup yogurt

Fish and Poultry: at least 3-4 servings per week
- 3 oz fish (about the size of a deck of cards when cooked)

- 3 oz poultry cooked with skin removed (about the size of a deck of cards when cooked)

Eggs: 1-2 servings per week
- 1 whole egg
- 2 egg whites

Heart Healthy Fats: 2-3 servings per day
- 1 teaspoon liquid oil
- 2 teaspoons butter-flavored spread (look for those with no transfatty acids)

Nuts and Legumes: 1 serving of each almost every day
- 1 ounce of nuts (small handful)
- 2 tablespoons of peanut or other nut butter
- 1/2 cup cooked beans

After twelve weeks, you will have started to make the changes that will benefit you for the rest of our life. Remember, healthy eating should be a lifestyle choice, not simply a short-term test of willpower.

12. Weight-Loss Plan

Exercise, diet and overall wellness are inexorably intertwined. A weight loss plan that addresses both the exercise and nutrition sides of the equation is one that has a much better chance of success than a plan that attacks only one or the other.

Even the most faithful exercisers can cancel out the calories they burn through walking with a couple of large meals. See if this puts things in perspective...walking at a moderate pace for 60 minutes burns roughly 300 calories. An order of small French fries at McDonalds has 450 calories. You can see that it doesn't take much for the calories to add up.

"If I don't even burn off an order of fries, why should I even bother with exercising?" you might ask. In addition to all the physical and mental health benefits to walking, there is another important factor to be considered. Studies have shown that dieting without exercise can lead to a reduction in body fat, but the weight loss is usually from fat deep inside the body. On the other hand, when people lose weight through exercise, the reduction is from the fat just underneath the skin. This fat right underneath the skin has the biggest impact on how you look.

The Walking for Weight Loss Plan is really a matter of combining one of the Walking Plans outlined previously along with the healthy diet detailed in the Nutrition chapter. The key is to combine both diet and exercise in order to burn more calories than you consume.

Do You Need to Lose Weight?

Just like with walking, it's important to have a goal in mind when approaching weight loss. The first thing to do is figure out if you really need to lose weight. You can do that by calculating your Body Mass Index, or by having your Body Fat Percentage measured. Based off of those numbers, you can create short and long term weight loss goals.

BMI

Your BMI (Body Mass Index) is a good indicator of your body composition. You can calculate your BMI using the following formula:

BMI = 703/(height in inches x height in inches) x Weight in pounds

Remember, with mathematical equations you want to start with anything within parenthesis first. *Here is an example for Linda, who is 5'7" and weights 153 pounds.*

1. Determine height in inches.
5'7" is the same as 67 inches.

2. Multiple (height in inches x height in inches).
(67 x 67) = 4489

3. Take the number you calculated in step two and divide it into 703.
703/4489 = .156602

4. Take the number you calculated in step three and multiply it by weight in pounds.
.156602 x 155 = 24.3

5. Take the number you calculated in step 4 and compare it to the BMI classifications below.

24.3 falls within the "Normal Weight" category. Linda should be careful not to gain weight however, because she is quite near the upper end of the category.

Now, calculate your own BMI and record your category on today's date in your walking log. (If you don't feel like making the calculations and have access to the internet, there are hundreds of sites that will calculate your BMI for you. Try www.oxygen.com/tools/bmi/)

CATEGORIES AND YOUR BMI

Categories	Calculated BMI
Underweight	Less than 18.5
Normal Weight	18.5 – 24.9
Overweight	25 – 29.9
Obese	30 or greater

Be aware that the BMI formula may overestimate body fat in athletes and others who have a muscular build. In addition, it may underestimate body fat in older persons and others who have lost muscle mass.

Body Fat Percentage

An even more accurate indicator of your body composition than your BMI is your overall percentage of body fat. You can have your body fat tested at most gyms and some hospitals for a small fee. Healthy body fat percentages for women fall between 20-35%, with the average being about 28%. The healthy range for men is 8-22%, with the average about 15%.

> ### IGNORE YOUR SCALE
> Weight is not the most accurate indicator of how fit you are. Because lean muscle weighs more than fat, somebody who weighs more than you might actually be fitter and wear smaller clothes. Don't use your scale to chart your progress. Look to your body fat percentage, your waist size, or even how your clothes fit to gauge whether you are making headway.

Plan Overview

If your goal is to lose weight, a sensible approach is to cut 250 calories per day from your normal eating routine and then burn 250 calories per day through exercise. That 500 calorie-a-day deficit leads cutting 3500 calories over the course of a week. It just so happens that one pound of body fat is equivalent to 3500 calories. By cutting 250 calories a day through your eating habits and burning 250 calories a day through exercise, you will lose a pound a week.

Remember, we're taking a long-term approach to wellness here. This is not a book about crash dieting and "get fit quick" schemes. Averaging weight loss of about a pound a week is a healthy and attainable objective.

THE FOOD SIDE OF THE EQUATION
Calories In vs. Calories Out

At the end of the day, weight loss comes down to a simple formula. It's "calories consumed" verses "calories burned." If you burned more calories than you consumed in a day then, over time, you'll lose weight. The problem is that counting calories is too much work for some people. It can be time consuming and cumbersome to calculate the caloric value of everything that passes your lips.

The good news is that most people don't have to count calories to lose weight. By making some simple shifts and substitutions in your eating habits, you can cut 250 calories a day without really thinking about it.

You can read about the most important changes to make to your diet in the Nutrition for Healthy Walkers chapter. Some of the best changes outlined in that chapter for cutting calories include:

- Switch to Low Fat and Skim Dairy Products
- Substitute Whole Grains for Refined Ones
- Emphasize the Sides
- Have a Restaurant Strategy
- Substitute Water and Juices for Alcohol and Soda
- Eat Heart-Healthy Fats
- Learn Your Serving Sizes

You don't want to try to make all the changes at once. Incorporate them gradually into your regular eating plan so that they become part of how you eat for the rest of your life.

OTHER EASY WAYS TO TRIM THE FAT
- Use low sugar jelly instead of cream cheese
- Sautee food in broth or wine instead of oil
- Use fat free or low fat salad dressing and mayonnaise
- Use herbs and spices to season foods instead of oil or butter
- Try not to eat much fried food

Figuring out Why and When You Overeat

Some people are overweight because of poor eating habits that have led to a diet high in fatty and sugary foods. Others have become overweight because they use food to make them feel better. They may turn to food as a "cure" when they are unhappy or under stress. Others see food or maybe empty calorie alcohol as an integral part of socializing. It's important for you to understand patterns in your eating habits in order to help yourself avoid situations where you are prone to overdoing it.

One easy way to do this is keep a food journal. For four days, including a Friday and Saturday night, write down everything you eat. Then, just as important, write down how hungry you were when you ate and exactly why you ate. You may find that you tend to overeat when you let yourself get starving. If that's the case, you can make sure you have healthy snacks around so that you don't ever let yourself get ravenous. You may see that you turn to food as a release when you're under stress. Instead of letting that happen, you can take a walk to help yourself unwind.

Many people eat healthily during the week and then go crazy on the weekends. An occasional free-for-all isn't going to derail your nutrition plan, but if it's a weekly occurrence it will be hard for you to drop the pounds. If you see that you're only overeating after you've had a few drinks, you should consider cutting back on alcohol. If you always go out to dinner as a way of hooking up with your friends, maybe you can all go for a hike instead. There are always alternatives.

Pay Attention When You Eat

In today's fast paced world, we always seem to be multi-tasking. You can do yourself a big favor by concentrating wholly and fully on eating when you have food in front of you. You will savor every bite, which may help you feel satisfied sooner, and you will be able to hear your body tell you that you're full.

Studies have shown that people consistently eat more when they are watching TV or doing something else in addition to focusing on their meal. That means no eating in front of the television or while you're working at your desk. Instead, focus on the flavors of what you are eating. Chew slowly and enjoy the process.

THE EXERCISE SIDE OF THE EQUATION

Our goal with this plan, in addition to cutting 250 calories a day from our diets, is to burn 250 additional calories a day through exercise. If you're currently not on any type of exercise program, that means adding a daily walk that burns 250 calories. If you are already exercising, you'll need to crank up the duration, frequency, or intensity of your program in order to burn those extra 250 calories.

What It Takes

Just what does it take to burn 250 calories a day through exercise? If you're walking at a moderate pace, fast enough to walk one mile in 15 minutes, you will burn 250 calories after about 50 minutes. If you increase your speed to walk a 13-minute mile instead, you only need to walk for 40 minutes.

If you haven't been exercising, you need to work your way up to 50 minutes slowly. Begin with the Starter Plan and then move along to the Walking for Health Plan. As another alternative, you can try to 10,000 Steps Plan outlined below.

10,000 Steps Plan

One of my favorite ways to make sure I'm getting enough movement on a daily basis is to wear a pedometer all day long. I check my pedometer every couple of hours to see how I'm doing, which motivates me to think of ways to take more steps. For example, I changed my default printer at work so that all my papers come out on a printer downstairs. That way I have to walk up and down a flight of stairs every time I print something. I also always use a restroom far away from my office, instead of the one right next door.

If evening rolls around and I haven't gotten all my steps I'll resort to desperate measures, like vacuuming the whole house or mowing the lawn. If I go to the grocery store and I still need steps, I'll park in the spot furthest away from the store and then walk all the aisles.

If you're trying to slim down, I suggest working towards a goal of 10,000 total steps every day. That's the equivalent of about five miles. You'll put your pedometer on when you get dressed in the morning and then wear is all day until you go to bed.

As with any exercise plan, you should start moderately. Start by wearing the pedometer every day for a week, but don't modify your normal routine in any way. Take an average of the number of steps you took per day. This will be your starting point. Then, try to add 20% a week until you get to 10,000 steps.

For example, you might find that following your regular routine for a week you average about 4,000 steps a day. Your goal the next week should be 4,800 steps a day. (4,000 x 1.2) The next week you'll aim for 5,800, then 7000, and so on until you reach 10,000 steps a day.

A daily walk is obviously one of the best ways to get your steps in. Be sure the write down the number of steps you take per day in your walking log so that you can track your progress. (See "Accessories, Gadgets and Gizmos" in the Getting Started chapter for information on buying a pedometer.)

13. Issues for Women

Women are more prone to being the victims of crime while they are walking. In addition, women's bodies go through some special stages that men's don't. Some of these stages affect the ways you can exercise. I'll cover both of these subjects in this chapter.

Personal Safety

Women, unfortunately, are generally more vulnerable in terms of personal safety than men. That doesn't mean we shouldn't get out there and walk, but we need to be careful. Here are some precautions that we can take. (Men, by the way, would do well to take these precautions too.) Don't get too freaked out about your susceptibility, but do take the proper steps to ensure that you're a safe as you can be.

Before You Go

Some of the best safety insurance happens before you leave home:

- Let somebody know when you are leaving, where you are going, and when you expect to be back.

- Think about carrying a cellular phone so that you can call somebody at the first sign of trouble. If you don't carry a phone, make sure that you know where any phones are located along your route.

- Make sure you have something with you that identifies your name, phone number, an emergency contact, and any important medical information. It can even be a piece of paper stuffed in your shoe, but it's important to have.

- Walk with a friend or a dog for a little extra protection.

Stay Alert and Aware

Another way to avoid trouble is to be aware of the first sign of it. The University of Texas Police Department offers some of the following tips for walkers:

- Be alert to your surroundings. Even though it's easy to go off into a "walking trance," try to check in and make sure that everything and everybody around you looks okay.

- Walk confidently, directly and at a steady pace. Attackers look for someone who appears vulnerable.

- Be aware of places along your route where somebody might be able to hide (behind shrubbery for example) and avoid those spots.

- Don't wear headphones. They can drown out the sound of an approaching car or person until it's too late.

- Stay on well-lit routes so that you can see anybody that might be around you. Routes with people and activity are preferable to unpopulated, deserted stretches.

- Walk facing traffic so that you can see who's in each car and so that it's harder for somebody to drive up behind you.

- Notice parked cars along your route and stay clear of them by a few yards.

Pay Attention to Instinct

It's definitely a good idea to follow your intuition when it comes to personal safety:

- If you think you are being followed and you feel threatened, head for the nearest populated place, be it a store, theater, or even an unknown person's lighted house.

- Be wary if anybody in a car stops to ask you something. Always stay a few arm's lengths away from the car door.

- If a person or area just doesn't "feel right," pay attention to that instinct and get away from there.

LIFE STAGES
I. PREGNANCY

During pregnancy your body undergoes tremendous changes. That means you've got to make adjustments to your exercise regime. Exercise is still very important however. Women who do some form of moderate exercise during pregnancy generally gain less weight, sleep better, feel better, and, most importantly for some, get the weight off faster postpartum. Walking is an excellent option.

Precautions

There are quite a few precautions that need to be taken when exercising when pregnant. The first and most important thing is to get your doctor's okay. You might have a high-risk pregnancy that makes it best not to exercise during this time, so getting your doctor's approval is paramount.

After your doctor has given you the all clear, you'll still need to be careful. Probably the best advice is to listen to your body. It is busy creating a little human being, so it may not be able to do some of the things it has done in the past. If you ever feel weak, tired, or any pain, you should stop immediately. Never during pregnancy should you exercise so hard that you are exhausted or out of breath. Both overheating and dehydration should be avoided at all costs. That means no walking in extremely hot or humid weather as well as taking lots of drinking breaks.

During pregnancy your body releases hormones that make your joints looser to help accommodate your growing baby. In addition, all that extra weight shifts your center of gravity, throwing off your balance. Unfortunately, that means you're more prone to sprains and strains, especially ankle and knee injuries, during this time. Take care to walk on smooth, stable ground when you are pregnant, avoiding rocks and roots. You'll also want to make sure that your shoes offer plenty of ankle and arch support.

HELL HATH NO FURY LIKE THE HUNGRY PREGNANT WOMAN

When you're pregnant your body uses carbohydrates much more quickly than it normally does. While exercising, carbohydrates are also a main source of fuel. Combine the two, and you have the potential for a low blood sugar crash. That can lead to one very hungry, cranky, and weak pregnant woman. It's important that you carry a snack with you while walking to avoid this situation. Tune into your body and take a break to eat whenever you start to feel hungry or a little shaky.

Programs

If you were on a regular walking program before you got pregnant, and your doctor says its okay, you should be able to continue your program with some modifications. It's best during this time to keep your heart rate at a moderate level. That means that conversation should not be difficult when you walk. You probably don't want to increase the amount of time you walk either. Just maintain or cut back to a level that doesn't wear you out.

You might find as you get further into your pregnancy that the impact of walking becomes too much. At that time I recommend swimming as a nice, buoyant alternative.

If you weren't a regular exerciser before pregnancy, you'll want to be very careful about starting a new program. Have your doctor recommend a plan and then take it very slowly.

Post-Delivery

Having a new member in your household will shake up all your normal routines. The demands and stresses of taking care of an infant, including disrupted sleep, lack of time, and loss of energy, might make a walking program seem like an impossible task. Studies have shown however, that women who participate in postpartum exercise return more quickly to their pre-pregnancy weight, have more energy, and feel less stress.

That doesn't mean that you hop off the delivery table and start a program however. Once again, your doctor's approval is key here. Many doctors advise waiting six weeks after a normal delivery and even longer if you had a C-section or a complicated birth before resuming exercise.

New information shows that your joints will stay loose for up to four months after delivery, so you'll need to take the same precautions that you did while pregnant to avoid strains and sprains. You'll want to start back into your walking program gradually and again, pay attention to the signals you're receiving from your body.

Many women are anxious to lose weight after having a baby, but keep in mind that a reasonable goal for weight loss is no more than a pound per week. (See the Walking for Weight Loss chapter for information on losing weight this way.) If you're breast-feeding also be aware that your body will cling to those last ten pounds as insurance that you won't leave your baby hungry. Recognize this and feel comfortable with the fact that you'll just have to wait until your baby is weaned to fit into those pre-pregnancy jeans.

Once you're feeling up to it, you can pick out the appropriate walking program in this book based on your current fitness level and go for it.

II. MENOPAUSE

Walking is a wonderful remedy to many of the increased risks of disease and symptoms that come with menopause. As you approach menopause your body starts to secrete less estrogen. This decline in estrogen levels makes your more prone to developing heart disease. Regular aerobic exercise, like walking, has been shown to greatly increase women's cardiovascular fitness and reduce the risk of heart problems. The lower levels of estrogen in your system can also lead to increased risk of osteoporosis. Weight bearing exercise like walking is the perfect antidote to this as it preserves bone mass in the spines of postmenopausal women, helping reduce fractures. Some mood and sleep disturbances are also related to estrogen deficiency. Once again, regular aerobic exercise, like walking, has been shown to enhance mood and facilitate sleep in menopausal women, even reducing night sweats.

Older women also have a tendency towards a loss of muscle tissue and strength. Unfortunately, this lean mass is usually replaced by an accumulation of fat. Both walking and resistance training are paramount in reversing this trend. Overtime women's muscles also tend to lose elasticity. Activities like yoga, pilates, and even simple stretching are the best solutions to this problem.

You can see that a walking program, combined with resistance training and stretching, has both a short-term and long-term component. In the short-term, an exercise program will help eliminate the symptoms and reduce this risks of disease brought about by menopause. But, just as importantly, an exercise program can help postmenopausal women maintain a high quality of life into their later years. Obviously a strong, mobile woman will have the ability to remain independent and take care of herself for many years to come.

You'll want to consult with your doctor before you start any exercise program, but with his or her okay you can use the appropriate walking plans in this book to help lead a healthier life.

14. Walking Clubs

If you enjoy the camaraderie of walking with others and are looking for a walking group to join, you should check out your local chapter of the **American Volkssport Association**. There are hundreds of affiliate clubs in the United States and thousands around the world.

Local clubs host many walking events. These are not pledge walks or races, but rather fun walks you do with the club. The club members select trails for safety, scenic interest, historic areas, natural beauty and walkability. They then invite everyone to come and enjoy the trails on weekends or weekday evenings. The trails are marked or maps provided. Trails may be in cities, towns, parks, forests, rural areas, anywhere there is a pleasant or interesting place to walk.

You can contact the association at:

American Volkssport Association
1001 Pat Booker Road
Suite 101
Universal City, TX 78148
Tel. (210) 659-2112
Fax (210) 659-1212
Information Line 1-800-830-WALK

A partial listing of clubs can be found below. A full listing of local clubs and other useful information can be found on the association's website: www.ava.org.

ALABAMA
Capital City Wanderers
PO Box 210911
Montgomery, AL 36021
Robin Grantham, Tel. (334) 514-0948
E-Mail: rovinggrantham@compuserve.com

ALASKA
Anchorage Volkssport Club
P.O Box 202298
Anchorage, AK 99520-2298
J Michael Devitt, Tel. (907) 271-4348/338-4025
E-Mail: jmdevitt@alaska.com

ARIZONA
Tucson Volkssport Klub
270 S. Candlestick Dr
Tucson, AZ 85748-6743
Fred Barton, Tel. (520) 298-4340
E-Mail: mount@bird.library.arizona.edu

Valley Volkssporters Association
101 N 38th St #30
Mesa, AZ 85205-8526
Hal Witter, Tel. (480)641-7577

ARKANSAS
Arkansas Octoberfest Volksmarsch
PO Box 1860
Hot Springs, AR 71902-0000
Gail Sears, Tel. (501) 624-3383
E-Mail: gail_sears@nps.gov

CALIFORNIA
Bay Bandits Volksmarch Club
PO Box 422815
San Francisco, CA 94142-2815
James Yakas, Tel. (415) 334-4279
E-Mail: SFBayBandits@aol.com

Big Valley Vagabonds
4825 N. 5th
Fresno, CA 93726
Glenda Butterfield , Tel. (559) 229-0906
E-Mail: gwbutterfield@aol.com

California Volkssport Assn.
2850 Gayle Lane
Auburn, CA 95602-9674
Herb Webber, Tel. (530) 878-7023
E-Mail: herbw@jps.net

Sacramento Walking Sticks
PO Box 191834
Sacramento, CA 95819-7834
Myrna Jackson, Tel. (916)481-6714
E-Mail: gon2wok@cwnet.com

San Diego County Rockhoppers
2525 A Jefferson St.
Carlsbad, CA 92008
Denyce Kinkead, Tel. (760) 720-3773
E-Mail: dkinkead@juno.com

COLORADO
Colorado High Country Hikers
31062 Wildwoods
Evergreen, CO 80439-0000
David Johnston, Tel. (303) 674-0317
E-Mail: dave@johnston.net

Colorado Springs Walking Club
2864 Dublin Blvd # 365
Colorado Springs, CO 80918
Lynette Reagan , Tel. (719) 532-0930
E-Mail: Lynnwalks@earthlink.net

Northern Front Range Wanderers
PO Box 271683
Ft Collins, CO 80527
Hugh Metcalf, Tel. (970) 207-0267
E-Mail: hemetcalf@aol.com

CONNECTICUT
Connecticut Valley Volkssport Club
PO Box 251
Glastonbury, CT 06033-0251
Bob Mcdougall, Tel. (860) 342-3062
E-Mail: mcdougall@encompasserve.org

DELAWARE
First State Webfooters Walking Club
PO Box 1949
Dover, DE 19903-1949
Hazel Meegan, Tel. (302) 947-1254
E-Mail: hazelmeegan@webtv.net

DISTRICT OF COLUMBIA
Mid-Atlantic Walking Assoc
5605 Asbury Ct
Alexandria, VA 22312-6302
Diane Howell Evans, Tel. (703) 354-1735

Washington Dc Area Volksmarch Club
PO Box 3432
Merrifield, VA 22116
Diane Evans, Tel. (703) 354-1735

FLORIDA
Florida Volkssport Assn

2975 Wild Pecan Ct.
Port Orange, FL 32129-6200
Marvin Stokes, Tel. (386) 788-4026
E-Mail: marvst37@earthlink.net

Panama City Volksmarchers
PO Box 10121
Panama City, FL 32404-1121
DJ Moore, Tel. (850) 871-2624
E-Mail: tyc49@knology.net

Pensacola Volksmarch Club
PO Box 30024
Pensacola, FL 32503-1024
Dick Wonson, Tel. (850) 623-3939
E-Mail: nellee@pcola.gulf.net

Tallahassee Volkssport Club
3679 Barbary Drive
Tallahassee, FL 32308
Lawrence Tepe, Tel. (904) 668-0565
E-Mail: brownr@dms.state.fl.us

GEORGIA
International City Volkssport Association
PO Box 237
Perry, GA 31069
Stephen Weigandt, Tel. (912) 987-8501
E-Mail: intcityvolksassn@web-unwired.net

HAWAII
Menehune Marchers
PO Box 31102
Honolulu, HI 96820-0000
Dawn Miyashiro, Tel. (808) 536-1654
E-Mail: maria.brasher@eudoramail.com

IDAHO
Treasure Valley Volkssports

3033 E Rivernest Dr
Boise, ID 83706
Juliann Fritchman, Tel. (208) 345-8259

ILLINOIS
Illinois Volkssport Assn
3109 Valerie Drive
Champaign, IL 61821
David Bradley, Tel. (217) 355-6811
E-Mail: dybradley@aol.com

Railsplitter Wanderers
PO Box 6051
Springfield, IL 62708-0000
Bruce Vanderkolk, Tel. (217)787-8184

INDIANA
Hoosier Hikers
PO Box 11101
South Bend, IN 46634-0000
Robert A. Buzolich - 219-233-4441
E-Mail: sonofbuzz@prodigy.net

Indiana Volkssport Assn., Inc
6330 Woods Edge N. Dr # 2-B
Indianapolis, IN 46250
Don Vartanian, Tel. (847) 843-0212
E-Mail: donvart@att.com

IOWA
Greater Des Moines Volkssport Assn
PO Box 110
Des Moines, IA 50301-0110
Phyllis Olson, Tel. (515) 270-6920
E-Mail: paolson@home.com

KANSAS
Heart Of America Volkssport Assoc
11711 W 100 Terr

Overland Park, KS 66214
Dick Haverkorn, Tel. (913) 492-5382

KENTUCKY
Derby City Walkers
1363 Tyler Park Dr
Louisville, KY 40204-1539
Herb Zimmerman, Tel. (502) 456-6126
E-Mail: bedharris@aol.com

LOUISIANA
Baton Rouge Striders Assn
618 Cockerham Rd
Denham Springs, LA 70726
Barbara Porche, Tel. (225) 261-4279

Crescent City Volkssport Club
605 North Alexander St
New Orleans, LA 70119
Brian Winters, Tel. (504) 482-4315

MAINE
Southern Maine Volkssport Assn
PO Box 722
Westbrook, ME 04098-0722
Dan Carr, Tel. (207) 929-4047
E-Mail: seejohnrun@cybertours.com

Wandering Maine-Iacs
PO Box 6403
Portland, ME 04102-6403
David Muzzy, Tel. (207) 854-5424

MARYLAND
Baltimore Walking Club
7905 Omega Ct
Kingsville, MD 21087
Bill Simmons, Tel. (410) 592-8440
E-Mail: FKupres@home.com

Maryland Volkssport Assn
7861 Poplar Grove Rd
Severn, MD 21144-2025
Ron Looper, Tel. (410) 969-8661

MASSACHUSETTS
Walk 'N Mass Volkssport Club
5 Kent Drive
Hudson, MA 01749-1113
Ernest Lavoilette, Tel. (978) 562-7023
E-Mail: elavio@rcn.com

MICHIGAN
Mackinaw Walkers Volkssport Club
1706 Pine
Belleville, IL 62226-4256
Jim Muma, Tel. (618) 234-8706

MINNESOTA
Central Minnesota Volkssports
P.O. Box 2162
St Cloud, MN 56302-2162
Richard (Dick) Ditrich, Tel. (320) 253-6595

Minnesota Volkssport Assn
2659 - 139th Lane NW
Andover, MN 55304
Martha Stellmach - 763-755-8741
E-Mail: pdstachour@uswest.net

MISSISSIPPI
Magnolia State Volkssport Club
PO Box 731
Biloxi, MS 39533-0731
Neal Gambler, Tel. (228) 872-3059

MISSOURI
Clay-Platte Trackers
7332 N. Oakland Ave

Kansas City, MO 64158
Marty Burke, Tel. (816) 781-7881
E-Mail: eburke@kc.rr.com

St Louis-Stuttgart Sister City
6700 Arsenal Street
St Louis, MO 63139
Roy E Leimberg, Tel. (314) 863-7045

MONTANA
Helena Hikers
Box 2248
Clancy, MT 59634
Roy Hockett, Tel. (406) 443-7010

NEBRASKA
Lincoln Volkssport Club Inc
PO Box 83704
Lincoln, NE 68501-3704
Rose Quackenbush, Tel. (402) 464-6972

NEVADA
Las Vegas High Rollers & Strollers
PO Box 20768
Las Vegas, NV 89112-2768
Joseph Lepire, Tel. (702) 456-9944
E-Mail: dicklisk@lvcm.com

Sierra Nevada Striders
PO Box 3542
Reno, NV 89505-3542
Laurie Dinsmore, Tel. (775) 677-2259
E-Mail: snstriders@worldnet.att.net

NEW HAMPSHIRE
Granite State Trail Walkers
PO Box 133
Jaffrey, NH 03452-0000
Patty Proulx, Tel. (603) 532-7472

Seacoast Striders
PO Box 3151
Portsmouth, NH 03802-0168
Claudia Cauchon, Tel. (603) 659-8598/862-1533

NEW JERSEY
Garden State Wanderers
19 Misty Pine Lane
Hamilton Square, NJ 08690-0000
Vasily Serpikov, Tel. (609) 587-5251

Princeton Area Walkers
7 East Wilson Circle
Red Bank, NJ 07701-5829
Donna C. Coulson, Tel. (732) 758-8191

NEW MEXICO
Albuquerque AVA Amigos
3519 Hannett Ave. NE
Albuquerque, NM 87106-1116
Meg Gregory, Tel. (505) 265-3839
E-Mail: meggregory@principa.edu

Santa Fe Trail Blazers
3008 Cliff Palace
Santa Fe, NM 87505-0000
Frank Demolli - 505-473-7991
E-Mail: SFSChief@aol.com

NEW YORK
Empire State Capital Volkssporters
PO Box 5464
Clifton Park, NY 12065-5464
Dave Golden, Tel. (518) 371-0604
E-Mail: EFSkinner@aol.com

Niagara Escarpment Volkssport Assoc
2181 Violet Circle Apt 1
Niagara Falls, NY 14304-2901

Dorothy N Socie, Tel. (716) 731-2630
E-Mail: TPJD123@aol.com

*Long Island Walkers Club
Lenny Kronski
E-mail: lennykro@aol.com

*New York Road Runners Club (also serves walkers)
New York Road Runners
9 East 89th Street
New York, NY 10128
Tel. (212) 860-4455
E-Mail: webmaster@nyrrc.org.

*Westchester Trails Association,
632 Warburton Ave., Apt 6-K, Yonkers, 10701
Linda Heilmann

NORTH CAROLINA
Metrolina Walkers
6360 Forest Way Dr
Charlotte, NC 28212
John Miles, Tel. (704) 586-7309
E-Mail: mail@metwalk.freeservers.com

Triangle Trailblazers
PO Box 90591
Raleigh, NC 27675-0591
Dawn Cassara, Tel. (919) 929-2346
E-Mail: mollytaylor@juno.com

NORTH DAKOTA
Bismarck-Mandan CVB
PO Box 2274
Bismarck, ND 58502
Julie Kotsick, Tel. (800) 767-3555

Note: the clubs above preceded by an asterisk are not part of the American Volkssport Association.

Red River Volkssport Assn.
109 Woodland Drive
Fargo, ND 58102
Ruth Herman, Tel. (701) 232-7258
E-Mail: rmherma@aol.com

OHIO
Heart Of Ohio Hikers
599 Lummisford Lane N.
Columbus, OH 43214
Max Rhoades, Tel. (614) 451-2905
E-Mail: mrhoades@cas.org

Ohio Volkssport Assn
705 Southwest 18th Street
Richmond, IN 47374
Thelma Goris, Tel. (765) 966-0391
E-Mail: thelmajg@infocom.com

OKLAHOMA
Frontier Walkers, Inc.
PO Box 2103
Oklahoma City, OK 73101-2103
Meredith Long, Tel. (405) 721-4201
E-Mail: mjlong@cox.net

Green Country Wander Freunde, The (Tulsa Walking Club)
PO Box 701856
Tulsa, OK 74170-1856
James Renner, Tel. (918) 251-7605

OREGON
Cedar Milers
1820 SW Huntington
Portland, OR 97225
Fran Swanson, Tel. (503) 643-2648
E-Mail: Swanso@easystreet.com

Columbia River Volkssport Club
9325 SW 190 Ave
Beaverton, OR 97007-6733
Richard Koonce, Tel. (503) 649-7675
E-Mail: Purpprez@teleport.com

PENNSYLVANIA
Penn-Dutch Pacers Volksmarch Club
PO Box 7445
Lancaster, PA 17604-7445
Phil Allamong, Tel. (717) 786-2255
E-Mail: phil@solanco.com

SOUTH CAROLINA
No active clubs In South Carolina

SOUTH DAKOTA
Capital City River Ramblers
800 West Dakota
Pierre, SD 57501-0000
Karen Kern, Tel. (605) 224-7361
E-Mail: kkern@pierrechamber.com

TENNESSEE
Gatlinburg Hiking Club
Gatlinburg Of Tourism, 234 Airport Rd
Gatlinburg, TN 37738-0000
Sandra Donohoo - 423-436-2392

TEXAS
Colorado River Walkers
PO Box 13051
Austin, TX 78711-3051
JoAnn Fries, Tel. (512) 303-9505
E-Mail: joannwoolf@aol.com

Dallas Trekkers,Inc
PO Box 743813
Dallas, TX 75374

Bruce Fitch, Tel. (972) 235-9086
E-Mail: bfitch@ix.netcom.com

Houston Happy Hikers
10510 Tenneta
Houston, TX 77099
Charles Christal, Tel. (281) 498-1365
E-Mail: ChalesC@aol.com

Texas Volkssport Assn.
712 Ridge Street
Copperas Cove, TX 76522-3137
Kark Kittinger, Tel. (254) 547-1403
E-Mail: walkabout@hotmail.com

UTAH
Gadabout
3897 N 1050 W
Ogden, UT 84414-0000
Myra Tams, Tel. (801) 777-9542/782-8580
E-Mail: tams@xmission.com

VERMONT
Twin State Volkssport Assn
PO Box 907
Middlebury, VT 05753
Charlotte Phillips, Tel. (802) 462-2019)
E-Mail: cpwalkvt@together.net

VIRGINIA
Northern Virginia Volksmarchers
PO Box 7096
Fairfax Station, VA 22039-7096
Thomas Andrew, Tel. (703) 369-0268

Virginia Volkssport Assn
14402 William Carr Lane
Centreville, VA 22020-2813
Fred Lopez, Tel. (703) 631-8512

WASHINGTON
Capitol Volkssport Club
PO Box 977
Olympia, WA 98507-0977
Val Lance, Tel. (360) 491-9554

Emerald City Wanderers
PO Box 16221
Seattle, WA 98116-0000
Sam Bess, Tel. (206) 367-0728
E-Mail: shbess@aol.com

Spokane Valley Of The Sun Volkssport Club
N 5421 Drury Rd
Otis Orchards, WA 99027-0000
John Balzens, Tel. (509) 325-4044

WEST VIRGINIA
Riverfront Ramblers
PO Box 28
St Albans, WV 25177-0000
Karen Maes, Tel. (304) 727-2699

WISCONSIN
Madison Area Volkssport Assn.
5824 Lochinvars Trail
Marshal, WI 53559-9720
None Specified.

WYOMING
Casper Pathfinders
1301 Manor Drive
Casper, WY 82609-0000
Rita Livingston, Tel. (307) 237-8378

Appendix A:
Weekly Walking Log

Goal for Week: _____

	Date	Target Minutes, Miles or Steps	Actual Minutes, Miles or Steps	Route	Motivation Level (1-5)	Notes (how you felt, etc.)
Sun.						
Mon.						
Tues.						
Wed.						
Thurs.						
Fri.						
Sat.						

Body Mass Index or Body Mass Percentage _____

Improved Fitness Plan Only
Current 1-Mile Walk Time _____

Fitness Category _____

Goal 1-Mile Walk Time _____

Appendix B: Improved Fitness Plan Using Target Heart Rate Method

TARGET HEART RATE METHOD
Calculating Target Heart Rate
Remember, the Target Heart Rate method is for people who like precision and are willing to make calculations or buy gadgets.

Your target heart rate is calculated by determining your predicated maximum heart rate per minute. Your workout goals are then expressed as a percentage of your maximum heart rate. For example, your goal might be to work at a target heart rate that is 75% of your predicted maximum heart rate.

Here is the simple formula for determining your target heart rate. We will use Linda to work through the example.

1. Calculate your predicted maximum heart rate by subtracting your age from 220.

Age – 220 = Max

For 38-year old Linda, her predicted maximum heart rate would be 220-38, or 182.

2. Multiple the results of step 1 by your desired intensity level. The intensity levels in the Walking for Fitness plan vary from 40% to 80% of predicted maximum heart rate depending on the workout.

(Max) x (target %) = Target Heart Rate

For Linda, we will calculate her target heart rate for both 50% and 75% of max Remember, her Max, which we calculated in step 1, is 182.

182 x .50 = 91   91 beats per minute is 50% of her predicted max.

182 x .75 = 137   137 beats per minute is 75% of her predicted max.

3. So, if the plan called for Linda to walk at a Target Heart Rate of 50%, she would aim for a pulse of 91 beats per minute. If it called her to walk at 75%, she would work to get her heart rate up to 137 beats per minute.

MEASURING HEART RATE
Heart Rate Monitor
Once you have calculated your target heart rate, you still have to measure your heart rate while you are walking. The easiest, most accurate, and most expensive way to do this is to buy a chest strap heart rate monitor. You can get a good quality, simple heart rate monitor for about $50. All you do is place the strap around your chest and wear the watch monitor around your wrist. The chest strap sends signals to your watch monitor so that the watch monitor displays your current heart rate in beats per minute. You observe and modify your effort level as you are walking so that you stay within a few beats of your target heart rate.

For more information on buying a heart rate monitor, see "Accessories, Gadgets, Gizmos" in the *Getting Started* chapter.

Pulse
You can also measure your heart rate by simply taking your pulse as you are walking. You can take your pulse for an entire minute, but that gets very cumbersome. The easiest thing to do is divide your target heart rate (which you calculated above) by 6 to get a 10-second target rate.

Using a watch you will then find your pulse, either on your neck or your wrist, and count the number of beats in 10 seconds (start counting with the number zero). You will modify your effort level as you walk so that you stay within a few beats of your 10-second target rate.

When finding your pulse it's important to use your index and middle fingers, not your thumb. Your thumb is often not sensitive enough to feel it. You can measure your pulse either on the left side of your neck, in the groove to the left of and slightly above the Adam's Apple, or on the left half of your left wrist. Be careful if you are taking your pulse at your neck that you don't poke yourself in the neck as you are walking.

Using Linda again as our example, let's assume that the plan calls for her to walk at a target heart rate of 75% of her max. We calculated above that Linda's 75% target heart rate was 137 beats per minute. Linda doesn't want to count her pulse for an entire minute though, she only want to count it for ten seconds.

Ten seconds is 1/6 of a minute. So, to find her 10-second target pulse, she would divide 137 by 6. That comes to 23. When Linda is walking, she will find her pulse and count the number of beats in 10 seconds. If it is higher than 23, she will slow down a little. If it is lower than 23, she will speed up.

The Plan
The only difference between this and the Improved Fitness Plan is that you are using your heart rate to judge how hard you are working rather than your Perceived Exertion. Please read through the Improved Fitness Plan so that you understand all the components before performing the workouts and then make the following substitution.

Perceived Exertion	Target Heart Rate
4	50% of Max
5	50% of Max
6	60% of Max
7	70% of Max
8	80% of Max

Interval Training

Now that you have a strong base upon which to build, during the next month we will work on increasing your speed and improving your cardiorespiratory capacity through Interval Training. Interval Training means that you will increase your walking intensity for short periods of time during your workout. These bursts of speed get your metabolism burning as well as prevent plateaus.

In between intervals you will keep walking, but at a lower intensity. This is called recovery time.

Here's an example of an interval workout. In this workout you walk at a constant pace for 20 minutes, then do 5 two-minute intervals each followed by a two-minute recovery walk. After you finish the intervals you will return to 15 minutes of constant pace walking.

20 minutes THR = 50%

2 minutes at THR = 80% followed by
2 minutes at THR = 40%
for a total of 20 minutes

15 minutes THR = 50%

Intervals & Hills

For the last month of the walking for fitness plan you will increase the intensity of your intervals and throw in some hill workouts as well. Find a gradually inclined hill or set of hills that takes you between two to four minutes to cover from top to bottom. Walking hills not only increases the workload on your heart, but it's also a form of resistance training for your legs because you are lifting the weight of your own body up an incline.

Here's an example of a hill workout. In this workout you walk at a constant pace for 20 minutes, then walk up your hill at a high intensity and turn around and recover by walking back down the hill. You will walk up and down the hill (or hills) for a total of 25 minutes, then return to 15 minutes of constant pace walking.

20 minutes THR = 50%

Hill workout: Walk up hill at THR = 80; return and walk down hill at any comfortable pace. Repeat walking up and down hill for 25 minutes.

15 minutes THR = 50%

Index

Cold Spring Press

We offer bulk purchases at significant discounts. If you are interested in buying this book in quantity, contact us at the address below for more details.

Cold Spring Press
P.O. Box 284, Cold Spring Harbor, NY 11724
E-mail: Jopenroad@aol.com

If you enjoyed this book, we also offer *Secrets of Smart Running*, $10.95, now in its third revised edition; like this book, it's a step-by-step approach to running for health, fun, and beginners interested in training for races.

For US orders, include $4.00 for postage and handling for the first book ordered; for each additional book, add $1.00. Orders outside US, inquire first about shipping charges (money order payable in US dollars on US banks only for overseas shipments).